MW00715531

Porn King

**by
John Holmes**

Johnny Wadd, Inc.
Albuquerque, New Mexico

Copyright ©1998 by John C. Holmes and Johnny Wadd, Inc.
All Rights Reserved

Printed in the United States of America
No part of this book may be reproduced without
written permission from the publisher, except for
brief quotations embodied in literary articles or reviews.

Published by
Johnny Wadd Publications
8200 Montgomery Blvd. NE, Suite 210
Albuquerque, New Mexico 87109

ISBN 1-880047-69-1

The Legend Continues . . .

Before John died, he felt that because he had led such an extraordinary, unusual life, in which he truly was a landmark in American Society and American Filmmaking, it was his responsibility to candidly share his experiences of his life once and for all. Throughout his career there had been many tall tales told of John Holmes. Some of them John even created himself in the interest of keeping his private life a mystery. However, John knew that some-day he wouldn't be around anymore and this was his last chance. He left many cassette tapes and writings behind, hoping that someday his fans would know exactly who he was and how he came to be something that over 20 years ago had no place or title of being. However, after 30 years since his first film and having starred in over 2,000 additional films, John Holmes is undoubtedly the King of Porn.

Following the horrific experience of my husband's passing, and the event's that took place directly after, I became very disenchanted with people and society as a whole. I withdrew inside myself, figuring that people were only going to believe what they wanted to believe *anyway, so it didn't matter. The industry in which John had fought so hard and eventually died for had turned their backs on him before and after his passing. The other society in which I never quite fit, I was struggling with more than ever. I found myself lost between a world of pornography that I had once believed in and fit in, and society that as much as I tried to fit in, I was too stubborn to subdue to it's ways.*

In my heart I knew that it was my husbands wish to have his book, "Porn King," published. However, it wasn't his family's wish that the book be printed. So, between the aching emptiness in my soul, and the overwhelming feeling to not hurt those that John loved dearly, I decided that immediately after his passing was not the time for me to proceed in the publishing of his extraordinary story.

After many years of struggling with what I feel in my heart is my destiny to do, and in spite of any hurt feelings it might cause, I know that the time has come to share his story, as he told it, with the world.

Laurie Holmes

CHAPTER 1

I t took less than five minutes to get from the Men's Gym to the Art Building on the UCLA campus - unless I detoured through the Women's Gym. Then it took a lot longer. The Women's Gym was a good place to study, and a great place to get turned on. On the second floor, at the back of the building, was an outside walkway that stretched from one end to the other. No one ever came up there, it was always deserted. Yet the view was incredible, over-looking the huge swimming pool and grassy area bounded by high brick walls. Except for those rare days when the weather was bad, the pool and surrounding deck were almost always crowded with nubile coeds in clinging swim wear. Some took to the water like trained seals, playfully bounding in and out, before emerging exhausted along the sidelines. There they stood hands on hips, drawing attention to their rounded bottoms, flat stomachs and high, heaving breasts. Others took to the grass, sitting cross-legged on towels while massaging their young bodies to glistening with globs of lotion, or stretching out in seduc-tive positions to soak in the sun.

The entrance to the girl's locker room offered an even better view, particularly when the double doors swung open wide. From the corridor, it was impossible to see past the wooden half-doors that had been installed at eye level just inside. Opposite the entrance, however, was a stairway lead-ing to the second floor. By sitting midway up, on the sixth or seventh stair, it was easy to look over the half-doors. The panorama was ever changing and often spectacular. I'd of-ten eat my lunch on the steps, or spend my study hours there casually flipping through books that seldom got read. I never considered myself a voyeur. I didn't peek through windows or go on the prowl to catch glimpses of ladies in various stages of undress. I looked openly, enjoying the passing parade from near and afar. There weren't many girls taking gym classes at UCLA in 1965 that escaped my glances as they wandered into the showers. Few of them bothered to wrap themselves in towels.

Not a day passed that I didn't think about sex. In fact, my overactive libido had gotten me in trouble before, and it would again. I was about to start a new job, one that demanded absolute composure and concentration. For a few hours, at least, I had to keep my mind relatively free of everything sexual. That meant going directly to the Art Building without dawdling in the Women's Gym. I didn't need the tension. What I did need was the job, and I couldn't afford to screw it up.

The classroom door was closed and posted with a sign that read - DO NOT ENTER, but I went inside anyway. A pale, fleshy, middle-aged women with Lucille Ball hair and Cleopatra eyes was lying stone naked next to a potted lily on a wicker settee at the far end of the room, stretched out with one ample leg propped over a paisley print cushion, the other hanging over the side. If she noticed me, she didn't let on. Except for her surging breasts - two partially filled sandbags studded with backup lights - she remained deathly still. Not even the slightest eye movement or the fluttering of a heavily massacred lash. The twenty or so students who faced her at their easels ignored my arrival as well, thank God. With their backs to the door they probably didn't hear me. More likely, they were too engrossed in capturing the breathing still life on canvas. Only the instructor, a tall, flashy dresser who had GQ written all over him, turned in my direction. He approached looking somewhat quizzical.

"I'm the model," I said flatly.

"Of course," he replied. "You're Mr. Homes." He smiled faintly and checked his watch.

I tried to return his smile but one wouldn't come. "Looks like I'm early," I answered instead, trying to sound nonchalant. The attempt backfired as my throat suddenly turned dry. Either that or an errant heartbeat had escaped from the pounding in my chest and had gotten in the way. Instead of sounding like a mature 20-year old, which I definitely considered myself to be, I came across as a crackly-voiced, sputtering adolescent.

"Not at all," said the instructor, reassuringly. "We'll be breaking in a few minutes. You might as well get ready before Miss Nichols needs the room."

"The room" was a dimly lit storage area adjoining the classroom, little more than a windowless closet crammed with books, old files and canvases, some rolled and piled on makeshift shelves, others stretched on frames and stacked against the walls. The air inside was heavy with the smell of turpentine, linseed oil and paint, not a bad spot, actually, for anyone into breathing fumes. The stench was so strong in fact, that lighting a match could have been dangerous. A dusty fluorescent fixture supporting three tubular lights dangled from the ceiling, held by fragile chains. The one light that still functioned sent out a flickering bluish glow accompanied by static buzz.

The storage area was a poor substitute for a changing room, but not worth complaining about. The building's days were numbered, at least as far as the art department was concerned. An impressive new structure, the nine-story Dickson Art Center, was rising on the north side of the campus. Within a few months, beginning with the fall 1965 semester, classes would be held there.

Outside, the library chimes were signaling 2:00 o'clock. A sudden clatter in the next room, mixed with voices, told me the class was breaking. I found a hanger and quickly stripped down, removing everything I had on - shirt, jeans, shoes and socks, even my wrist watch - until I stood bare-ass naked among the file cabinets. An old bathrobe that looked and smelled as if it hadn't been washed since the year one was hanging on a hook. Luckily, I'd brought a clean towel with me from the gym, sandwiched between the covers of my notebook. No sooner had I wrapped it around my middle than the door to the storage room opened. There stood Miss Nichols, all 200-plus pounds of her, wearing a brightly flowered kimono that hung loosely over her shoulders, untied and open at the waist. The slightly parted fabric revealed a view infinitely more tantalizing than the one that had been on open display.

"They're waiting for you," she said wearily, moving inside.

I brushed past her mumbling a barely audible "thanks," my heart racing all over again at the urgency of her words. After spending time in the dingy changing closet, the classroom seemed uncomfortably bright. Natural light, sunlight, streamed through a wall of glass, which may have been ideal for the artists but not for me. My eyes have always been extremely sensitive to light, and water easily. (They turn red and ugly.) No way could I sit facing the windows, staring into the glare. There was another concern, an even greater one. The majority of students were girls in their late teens, very attractive California beach types. The thought of sitting before them with everything hanging out was embarrassing enough, but would I be able to control my often-overactive imagination? It would take considerable concentration on my part to keep from becoming aroused. In a moment I'd be asked to remove the towel from my waist, unless catastrophe struck.

I found myself almost wishing for something devastating to happen - an earthquake, hurricane, tidal wave - anything to delay the inevitable. The more I dwelled on the subject the more apprehensive I became. I could feel my scrotum tightening, and my stomach knotting up. What was I doing in this place? Why was I the only person in the room not wearing clothes?

Money, plain and simple. Money to eat, money to live, money for school. I'd been working for six months to save enough to attend UCLA, washing dishes and cars, waiting tables, taking odd jobs whenever and wherever I could. I had to keep coming up with ways to keep the money coming in. Modeling for a Life Drawing class wasn't the greatest job in the world, but it was one of the most interesting and the pay wasn't half-bad.

"It looks like we're ready to begin, Mr. Holmes," the instructor said, motioning for me to take my place on the high stool in the center of the room. In my absence, the students had rearranged their easels into a circular pattern, like theater-in-the-round. I made my way through them, nervously fingering the terry wrapping at my midsection to check that it was still in place, and sat with my back to the window, purposely facing the ugliest male in attendance.

The instructor followed on my heels. "Strike a pose that's comfortable for you," he said. "Once you're set you won't be able to move".

I positioned myself more squarely on the stool, resting one foot on a rung and bracing the other on the floor. Then I leaned over placing an elbow on my knee, sinking my chin into the cup of my hand. I looked like a poor substitute for Rodin's "The Thinker."

"That will do," commented the instructor without much enthusiasm. (Did I sense some impatience on his part, or was he beginning to annoy me?) "But haven't you forgotten something?" He added, "The towel. Just drop it on the floor. We'll use it as a prop in the exercise."

I stood reluctantly and loosened the towel letting it fall free. Exactly where and how it fell, heaped or in artistic folds, I don't remember and didn't much care. My mind was on the students and their reaction to my nakedness.

At this point in my life I wasn't quite sure whether the Almighty had blessed me or cursed me. I only knew that I was "different." And painfully sensitive. One crack, one sarcastic remark and I was ready to bolt out the door. There were no words, thank God, none that I could hear anyway. But I did detect muffled sounds about the room: a throat clearing, scattered murmuring. Or was that my imagination too?

No sooner had I removed the towel then I was back on the stool, trying to duplicate my earlier pose. In my eagerness to resume the crouched position I must have turned slightly, for when I looked up I was not facing the ugliest guy in the class; he was off to the right. What I found instead was a young lady with lustrous, long dark hair, penetrating eyes, and full, sensuous lips. She was seated on a low stool, her easel angled at her side, and she wore a paint-spattered smock that covered her blouse but offered little protection for the rest of her. And the rest of her was sensational! Her tight miniskirt riding up her thighs, her long smooth legs - and the shadowy recesses in between - made quite a show. Had she kept her legs motionless, the view would not have been quite so captivating. Although her feet were planted firmly together, her thighs seemed to pulsate, opening and closing like butterfly wings in super slow motion. She fanned them apart, then pressed them together. Spreading, closing, spreading: the movement was hypnotic. At times, her thighs opened so tantalizingly wide that it was almost possible to discern the dark patch under her skirt. She appeared to be wearing panties. Then, again, she did not. It's doubtful that any of the students saw what she was doing. She moved so slightly, so effortlessly in a subconscious way that it would have taken a prolonged, studied look to discover she wasn't sitting absolutely still. Even then, because of their vantage point, they could not have noticed anything more than the most subtle changing of positions.

I followed her every move, no matter how fractional, and as I stared past the inner reaches of her smooth thighs into the blossoming, uncertain shadows, I was drawn uncontrollably into a wild sexual fantasy. God, it was starting! A tingling sensation raced through my groin, fed by the powerful juices of some unseen current. I felt myself hardening and rising until a part of me was pointing directly into the darkened depths, straight as a ramrod, as if to say, "I want you!" If her movements went undetected, mine did not. My dimensions had altered drastically; creating a stir among the young artists who sat facing me. They turned from their easels and began to buzz. The murmuring encircled the room like "The Wave" in a football stadium.

"Did I miss the bell - or are we taking a break?" an authoritative voice asked rhetorically from somewhere behind me.

An uncomfortable silence followed as the students straightened on their stools and returned to work. I willed myself to soften, but the more I concentrated on that seemingly simple feat the more I stiffened and throbbed. I felt flushed. Beads of perspiration formed on my brow; my hands and crotch grew clammy, The air felt suddenly stifling.

I began breathing uneasily through my mouth, parching my lips. I wanted to lick them but I didn't dare, not with my eyes focused on her. In desperation, I shifted my glance to the back of the room, then upward toward the ceiling. Still haunted by the smoldering mental images, I began to count holes in the acoustical tiles. When that failed, I turned to a wall chart showing a sexless human form with its muscles exposed.

The discovery of the well-defined rendering had me wondering why I'd been accepted to model for the class. For that matter, Miss Nichols as well. As a prerequisite for Life Drawing, the students had to complete a tough course in anatomy - similar to one required for pre-med majors - in which they had to learn the names and locations of all the bones, muscles and tendons in the body. Miss Nichols's bones were much too padded to be a good subject. At 6' 3" and 175 pounds, I was lean and lanky. The only muscle I displayed - more openly than I'd intended - unfortunately wasn't illustrated on any anatomy chart.

Out of the corners of my eyes I saw the miniskirted girl signaling for the instructor. Then he was at her side and I overheard her say, "The model has moved his eyes, sir, and I'm trying to draw them." Her message was quickly passed on to me, along with a few reminders of his own that stopped just short of chastisement. His words had a chilling effect, just what I needed.

When I looked back at the girl, she had a playful smirk on her face. She was at it again. Now her legs were spread even farther apart, well beyond proprietary bounds. She didn't even bother to close them. This deliciously humpy number was playing games with me, deliberately trying to turn me on!

Somehow I made it through the rest of the session without embarrassing myself more than I already had. Then I was off the stool, reaching for the towel and whipping it on. No longer was it my exposed front side that concerned me. After sitting in one position for nearly an hour, I had the uneasy feeling that I resembled one of those flamed-cheeked African baboons.

"Next time we'll try a different pose," said a voice at my side. I turned to find the instructor clearing the area that had been my stage; he was working with several other students in straightening the room. After a slight pause, he looked up and said, "I think we'll have you standing - what do you think of that? With your long legs it should be interesting."

He'd already answered his question so I just nodded. I doubted seriously, however, that my legs would be much of a factor if the sitting proved to be as "interesting" as the last one.

"Oh, before you get away, Mr. Holmes, I have something for you." From the inside breast pocket of his designer jacket he retrieved an envelope that contained a voucher - not a check or cash, which I was expecting - and typed instructions that directed me to the cashier's window in the Student Union. The thought of having to trek halfway across campus for a few bucks before heading home depressed me, but not enough to postpone the long walk till another day. I wanted the money now. I needed to feel my fingers wrapping around it. That was a fact of life, my life. I can't remember a time when the promise of money hasn't been a driving force in me. One that has too often led to trouble.

I had only to dress quickly and be off. However, it didn't quite work out that way. No sooner had I stepped into my little cubbyhole, discarded the towel and reached for my pants than the door began to creek open, so slowly that I thought I'd neglected to shut it tightly. That wasn't the case. Through the crack I saw two long, shapely legs and a miniskirt. "I'll be right out," I said instinctively, turning to step into my pants. The next thing I knew the door was opening wider, then closing, and she was standing inside, smiling vaguely and looking me over from head to toe. "I forgot something," the girl said quietly. Her voice was soft and feminine, edged with a touch of desperation. In her hands she carried a small paint box and the canvas she'd been working on in class. At that moment, as I struggled with one of the pant legs, I couldn't have cared less about what she was holding. My eyes were on her gorgeous thighs, and my mind was filled with visions of gently fanning butterfly wings.

She leaned the framed canvas against the others that lined the wall, then stepped forward to place the paint box on one of the narrow shelves. As she brought her hand down, it grazed my exposed groin, rather accidentally, I figured, until it fell back again, this time lingering there. God, my classroom fantasy was coming to life! That and a flashback to the time when I dreamed of banging my sexy third grade teacher, Mrs. Pryor, in the cloakroom. I'd never made it with "Pussy" Pryor, as the kids jokingly called her, but here I was with very much her equal - a younger version, actually - in much the same secluded setting. "Careful how you handle that, darlin'," I warned. "It could get out of control."

She wasn't careful, and it did get out of control. Her craving for sex matched mine. We were two desperate animals in heat. We both knew what we wanted, and nothing could hold us back.

What are we doing? It was one thing to be naked in a dim campus closet with a knockout coed, and quite another to have her on her knees with her head buried in my crotch.

"I think we'd better make sure the door's locked," I gulped nervously.

She pulled away and looked up sharply. An impish grin crossed her face as she said, "And take away all the thrill?" I smiled back, knowingly. She wasn't the first girl I'd met who had been turned on by the threat of getting caught. It was like having sex in a car on Hollywood Boulevard in broad daylight. Not my idea of a hot time, but if that's the way she wanted it I was certainly primed to go along with her.

We went at it for a solid ten minutes, oblivious to our cramped surroundings, before she drew back her head and let out a low, choking moan. My hand clamped tightly over her mouth as a searing sensation flooded my groin, jolting me once, twice, again and again with such a driving, pounding force that we were left clinging limply to each other, struggling for air. A moment later she slipped quietly away without saying a word. I pulled up my pants and reached for my shirt. It wasn't on the shelf where I'd placed it earlier; it was under my feet, having fallen to the floor unnoticed. Clean and freshly pressed that morning, it was now trampled, wet and sticky in places and gave off an unmistakable aroma. I held it at arm's length, flapping it to dry. A few seconds of that and I gave up, put the shirt on, and flicked out the light. I'd already delayed much too long.

The race to the Student Union and back across campus to the bus station on Hilgard Avenue nearly did me in. I wasn't in the best of shape anyway, thanks to the steamy session in the changing room. My legs felt weak and wobbly; I needed time to rest and recharge. I got more than I bargained for at the bus station. Sometime between dropping my pants and cashing the voucher my regular bus had arrived and departed.

Having to take the bus each day infuriated me. It wasn't so much the ride as the wasted time. I had a car, a borrowed one that I drove to school. What I didn't have was a permit to park on campus. Without one, and the one hundred-dollar fee, I was forced to park two miles away. I could have walked the distance, I suppose, but that too would have eaten into my schedule. Five nights a week, I washed dishes at a small hotdog stand in Hollywood. I was due on the job by 4:30, which meant I had to hustle, not sit on bus benches.

The car belonged to my roommate, Linda, a magnificently put-together 22-year-old with a sharp mind and a quick wit. Linda was a real crowd pleaser, in more ways than one. When we first met, she was working as a secretary for a high rolling attorney in Hollywood. She was also on call for evening activities with her boss's clients, a money sideline she kept to herself during the earliest days of our friendship. Apparently, she enjoyed her evenings more than her days for she soon left the attorney's employ to concentrate on a less restricting career, one that put no demands on her shorthand and typing skills. Her office became the topless joints and clubs along the strip of Hollywood where she met an endless supply of horny men with money to spare. Linda's new occupation worked fine for me, too. With her days reserved for sleeping, she had little use for her car.

One day, following the Life Drawing class, I returned to our apartment to drop off the car before heading to the restaurant. Linda was waiting for me, anxious to talk. "Not now," I said, rushing. "I'm late for work."

"How would you like to make a hundred bucks?" she asked with a sly smile. I slowed down.

"What did you say?"

"One...hundred...dollars", she repeated, punctuating each word. "Quick and easy."

Money from Heaven. "Who do I have to kill?" I asked, facetiously.

"I met a guy last night who makes dirty films for colleges and stag parties. You know, the kind where they show two people getting it on."

"And?"

"Well, he wants me to be in one of his films. You and me. I told him we make a great team."

Linda and I weren't strangers in bed. Whenever she had a rare night off, we'd sleep together. She was totally uninhibited.

One hundred bucks! I could see myself driving onto campus with my permit and pulling into a parking space. It sounded too good to be true. Getting paid for a few minutes of sex with my roommate? Surely, there had to be a hitch. "Come on, who do I have to kill?" I repeated.

Clever, clever me. Where had I heard that line before? On television or in a movie, spoken by Clint Eastwood, John Wayne, Charles Bronson? They were words that pleased the silent majority of patriotic Americans who stood by the government's effort in Vietnam, and sent chills through the hearts of draft resisters and flower children who proclaimed, "Make love not war," and "Girls say 'yes' to boys who say 'no'."

Who do I have to kill? Six words spoken in jest, certainly without malicious intent. Words that would come back to haunt me in the years ahead.

It was close to 11:00 P.M. when the doorbell rang. Through the curtains in the glare of the porch light, I could see the shadowy figure of a man pacing nervously back and forth. He appeared short and grossly overweight.

Linda beat me to the door. She opened it and quickly stepped aside. "Come on in, Harry," she said, keeping her voice low. "I'm glad you made it."

"Why not?" the fat man replied as he struggled through the opening. He turned his bloated body slightly so as not to bang the equipment in his arms. He carried a large, battered suitcase, two long light standards, and a tripod.

"I was afraid you might have a little trouble finding this place," Linda replied.

"Trouble? Don't mention the word."

"You know what I mean, Harry. Sometimes my directions are..."

"Listen, I made it," he interrupted. Setting the equipment on the floor, he plopped into the nearest chair, letting out a great rush of air as he landed. For a moment, he leaned back, wheezing, looking out through heavily lidded eyes like a dog on the alert. "Stairs," he gasped, "you didn't tell me about stairs."

"I'm sorry, Harry," Linda apologized. "I wasn't thinking."

A hacking cough jolted Harry upright. He leaned over the edge of the chair, gagging, his enormous belly tugging between his legs, seemingly on the verge of throwing up. His eyes bulged and turned glassy; he grew flushed and sweaty. At last, he dislodged some foreign matter deep in his throat and brought it forward on his tongue, letting it rest between his thick, rubbery lips before wiping it away with a small, dirty rag from his breast pocket. That done he sighed agonizingly, mopped at his face, neck and hairless dome, and returned the rag to his shirt.

"Would you like some water?" Linda offered.

"No," Harry said, waving her off. He struggled to his feet. "I've got to get busy - it's getting late."

"I want you to meet John," said Linda. "He's the guy I was telling you about."

With all of his distractions, it is doubtful Harry had really noticed me, even though I was in the same small room, sitting directly opposite him on Linda's bed. At least, that was the impression I got when he turned my way.

He stared more at my crotch than at me. I was dressed so he couldn't see anything, but he kept quiet. I had a sinking feeling that Harry didn't approve, and the possibility of bringing in a substitute to work with Linda began crossing my mind. I hoped I was misjudging his lack of comment because I'd psyched myself up for the job. At the moment, getting on with it, and collecting my money, was all that I wanted. In the 30 or so hours since Linda had asked me to participate in Harry's little epic, I'd had time to think about what I was getting myself into. Having sex in front of someone didn't bother me; I'd "performed" before people before, but only women. The thought of having a man looking on was something else.

Linda had tried to ease my fears. "He's just a slob who works in a bar in Hollywood and sells stag films to people in back alleys," she had told me. "He's nothing but a big jerk... don't worry about him."

I wanted to believe Linda, but I was apprehensive nevertheless - until Harry walked in. The moment I saw him I knew I'd do just fine. Harry didn't qualify as anything quite human. How he felt about me was another matter.

"You've never seen anything like John in action, Harry," Linda prodded. "He'll have your eyes popping."

"Good, good," Harry drooled. "That I want to see." He tugged up his pants and waddled over to the battered suitcase, pulled out a roll of aluminum foil, then scurried toward the large, curtained window.

"I'll be in the bathroom," Linda whispered to me. "Don't do anything until I come out."

I remained on the bed to watch Harry unrolling large sheets of silver paper. "What are you doing?" I asked.

He drew the curtain aside and pressed his fat face to the glass, scanning the street below. Pulling back quickly, he began covering the panes with foil. "The lights are like beacons at night," he puffed. "If a cop drives by and sees them, he'll know what's going on up here." I knew that stag films were very popular, and highly illegal, but I wasn't prepared for what Harry was about to tell me. He couldn't have picked a worse time to start babbling. "The cops make it difficult," he said. "They bust in during a shooting and do you know what you get? Ten years, that's what. Armed robbery gets one year. Murder gets seven. Think about it."

I did. Harry was making me nervous. The numbers he tossed out so freely made the paltry sum I'd be collecting - and, indeed, everything else - seem incidental. I was so steeped in thought that I didn't notice Linda until she was standing beside me. She had changed into a beat-up terry cloth robe, and she smelled delightful. "Are you going to get undressed?" she asked, nuzzling my ear.

"What?" I stammered.

She looked at me oddly, raising an eyebrow. "You're not getting cold feet, are you?"

"Who me?" I asked, forcing a grin.

"Then come on. Harry's almost ready."

Over her shoulder I could see Harry shuffling around. He'd already set up the lights; now he was mounting an 8mm camera on the tripod. I kicked off my tennis shoes, unzipped my pants, pulled them down, and was working on my shirt when I felt her moist tongue slithering around my crotch. I became aroused immediately.

"Good...good," Harry cried. "That's what I need. Just keep it up...but get on the bed." He snapped on one light, then the other, flooding the room with a blinding glare. "Now the camera," he said. "Ready?"

"Ready," I muttered, hovering over Linda's waiting body. I wasn't quite sure what I'd do next, only that I was about to be in my first - and last - sex film.

Little did I know.

CHAPTER 2

August 8, 1944. As the Nazi war machine continued its devastating, march across Europe, leaving the Continent in flames, squadrons of Allied planes took to the skies above Cannes to begin their counterattack to recapture occupied Paris. On the homefront that August day, Americans were buying War Bonds, doling out ration stamps, working in defense plants and tending Victory Gardens. Students crowded high school gyms at lunchtime to demonstrate the latest dance craze, the jitterbug. In taverns and malt shops, jukeboxes blared <u>The Trolley Song, Swinging on a Star</u> and other Hit Parade favorites for a nickel a play. Moviegoers lined up to see <u>Since You Went Away</u> and <u>Going My Way</u>. GIs with crew cuts pasted pin-ups of Betty Grable, Rita Hayworth and Lana Turner in their lockers. Teenage girls in sweaters, knee-length skirts and bobby sox daydreamed of Frank Sinatra, Guy Madison and Van Johnson. <u>Oklahoma!</u> was Broadway's big show. And on a wooden table in the kitchen of a modest Ohio farmhouse in Pickaway County, my mother gave birth to her fourth child, a son: John Curtis Holmes.

No doctor was present at my introduction into the world, Only a strapping neighbor lady who acted as midwife. The woman had previously assisted in dozens of deliveries, but from her reaction, she'd never seen anything like the long, hairless infant she held in her arms. After a scrutinizing once-over, her first words were not the customary announcement of gender or well being but a disbelieving, "This baby has three legs and two feet." In the years to come, the midwife's remark would be repeated countless times over, in varying forms and degrees of excitement. Her off-the-cuff reference to my middle "leg" was surprising considering the puritan surroundings. Any other euphemism, even clinical, would certainly have shocked my poor mother. As it was, she could easily have been led to believe that her latest born was strangely deformed. Fortunately, she was in a semi-stupor at the time.

The little frame farmhouse belonged to Mother's folks, Carrie and John Barton, a hardy, hard-working, deeply religious couple who shared a love of the land and family; good, proud people guided by God rather than money and its rewards. The long hours they put in daily should have earned them more than self-satisfaction, yet they never complained. To their way of thinking, luxuries were playthings of the rich, of far less importance than the minimal necessities of life. In that regard they had everything they could possibly need. It mattered little that the "facility" wasn't located inside, or that the wood burning stove in the kitchen was their main source of heat when temperatures dropped to freezing. Or that running water came not from a faucet but from a pump that had to be primed.

For six days a week, from dawn till dusk, Grandmother Barton tended to chores in and around the house. She had more to keep her busy cleaning and preparing meals. In the spring, she planted crops in the family garden: sweet corn, peas, beans, tomatoes, squash and more. In the summer and fall, she set the kitchen steaming with bubbling kettles filled with harvest, to be stored in glass Mason jars for winter eating. And, always, there were pigs to slop, chickens to feed, and eggs to gather.

Grandpa Barton, a tall, fair-haired Scotsman with electric-blue eyes, worked for a local railroad company. Each weekday morning at sunrise he could be seen walking the short distance from the house to the tracks where he'd await the early train that would carry him through the lush Ohio Valley into the big city, Columbus, some eighteen miles to the west.

Sundays were devoted to churchgoing and rest. It was also the day when the Holmes kids came to visit, which often made relaxing difficult, if not impossible. We were a boisterous bunch, and a houseful. In addition to me, there were brothers William and Eddy, and sister, Ann. To help channel our energy, and keep us out of the grown-up's hair, mother kept coming up with tasks for us to do. If she wasn't sending us off to the railroad tracks to collect scraps of wood for the kitchen stove (which, thinking back, was like shooing us out on the freeway to play), she'd have us pulling weeds in the vegetable patch or cleaning the poultry pens. Each of the assignments wisely kept us out of doors, away from the house. If the truth were known, the plot to "keep the kids busy" was probably more for Mother's benefit than for Grandma or Grandpa, who seemed genuinely, delighted to have us underfoot. In fact, John Barton frequently took me aside to tell adventurous tales of his childhood as he cradled me in his arms on the porch swing. A strong bond had developed between us early on. Having been named after him probably had a lot to do with our close relationship. He was also pleased that I was "the spitting' image" of him as a boy, the only one of his grandchildren who had his fair hair and blue eyes. "If I'd had a twin brother when I was growing up," he'd remark with a disbelieving shake of his head, "he'd have looked exactly like you. Why, having you around is like turning back the clock." Then, poking a long finger in my ribs, he'd crack, "But don't let that get you down."

No such bond developed between any of the Holmes children and Father's side of the family, and for good reason: we rarely saw them. Nor was much ever said about them, at least in a complimentary way. Whenever one of their names came up, the word "hillbilly" always popped into the conversation. As for Father, well...Mother was always making excuses for him, especially when we'd go visiting. "Ed is finishing up a job today," she'd explain to her parents, making him sound conscientious. Most often, however, she used a sympathetic approach. According to Mother, her husband had more colds, sore throats and upset stomachs than a room full of kindergartners. She should have saved her breath. Everyone knew better, and they couldn't have cared less.

Edward Holmes was an average-sized man; around six feet tall, with dark hair and watery, red rimmed eyes, a poor excuse for a human being and even lower on the scales as a husband and father. He called himself a carpenter although he worked only when necessary, which meant when he was desperate for a drink. Whatever money he earned, every penny of it, slipped quickly through his fingers in Columbus' bars and liquor stores. Beer, more than anything, was his passion. Memories of my father are hazy, mainly because our time together was extremely limited. Aside from his drinking, which was constant, two things really stand out in my mind. My earliest remembrance is of an unshaven, sloppy and slobbery man with a horrible stench on his breath leaning over and kissing me. The other is that he secretly collected nudist magazines. One day, when I was no more than four or five, I came across a dog-eared issue of <u>Sunshine and Health</u> that he'd stuffed under an old cushion. By today's standards, the photos inside, mainly shots of undressed adults and children wandering happily along wooded trails, weren't explicit, not even the shot of a bare-breasted girl posed artfully on a sandy dune. Seeing everyone totally exposed in the out-of-doors, and obviously enjoying themselves, must have been quite a revelation to me. No one in our family dared go anywhere without covering up, not even from room to room.

The discovery was much too important to keep to myself. Mother was taking a nap on the couch. She'd come home early; she was not feeling well. Not wanting to awaken her, I tiptoed to the living room window and pressed the magazine, opened to the naked girl on the beach, against the glass. It wasn't long before some of the neighborhood children began to gather, pointing fingers and snickering as they strained to see. The next thing I knew, Mother was awake and standing over me. "What are you doing, John?" she asked, sternly.

"Nothing," I mumbled. Until then, I hadn't realized I was doing anything wrong. But Mother's sudden presence, and the sharp tone of her voice, had me shaking.

"We'll see about that!" she snapped. Snatching the maga-zine from my hands, she quickly thumbed through it, her eyes growing wider with each passing page. Then she slammed it to the floor and grabbed my shoulders, holding firm. "Where did you get that trash?"

I started to cry.

"Tell me!" she demanded.

Somehow, I managed to point across the room and say, feebly, "Over there." That wasn't good enough, apparently, because I soon felt her hand whipping my butt. It was one of Mother's rare outbursts, and one that discouraged me - for a few years, at least - from making a spectacle of myself over a naked lady.

Unfortunately, my experience had no effect whatsoever on my Father. Not that it really mattered. Leaving the old man behind was only one reason we looked forward to our weekly trips to the country. The biggest benefit by far was getting away from the crummy place we called home.

Columbus, Ohio, like all of America, had been devastated by the Great Depression of the 1930's. Most of the country had rebounded by the start of World War II, but Columbus still counted vast numbers of indigents, many destitute, liv-ing in makeshift shacks and shanties around town. A num-ber of the poor and homeless even took to sneaking into the basements of other people's homes at night for shelter. The crime rate was staggering, and climbing. In seeking a solu-tion to the problem, the city fathers decided to round up all the poor and contain them within the industrial section of town, where the slums were located. A cluster of three-story red brick buildings, covering four city blocks, were con-structed - providing jobs for some of the unemployed - and "The Project" was born.

From the outside, "The Project" looked like a prison; bar-ren, cold, uninviting. It didn't get any better on the inside. The rooms were minuscule, dreary little cubes with cardboard walls and squeaky wooden floors, insufficient lighting, and provide-your-own heating. In winter, temperatures within dropped so low that spilled milk froze before it could be mopped up. On hot summer days, the vile smell of uncollected garbage became so overpowering that even the flies wanted out.

The first six years of my life were spent in a cramped two-bedroom "apartment" (for want of a better word) in "The Project." Eddy, Ann and I shared one bedroom, Mother and Father, whenever he showed up, shared the other. Being the oldest, and most responsible of the children, William was assigned his own private domain, a corner of the living room next to the kitchen partition. By concentrating the needy and homeless within a few square blocks, the city officials must have figured they could keep a closer watch on the troublemakers. It didn't quite work out that way. Crime in the streets did drop, but incidents within the housing project began to flourish. In effect, "The Project" became a war zone complete with race riots, stabbings, beatings and occasional flying bodies tossed from upper floor windows. Human screams mixed with wailing sirens of police cars and ambulances, which arrived and departed, were heard with frightening regularity. There weren't may quiet moments. Most of the trouble took place during daylight hours when the adults were away, either at work, wandering around looking for work or, in my Father's case, scrounging drinks. (Even the ones who had no ambition whatsoever had enough smarts to break away whenever possible.) From 8:00 in the morning until 6:00 at night, the entire Project was literally run and owned by children - gangs of rowdy street-smart punks who'd rather crack heads than baseballs. One of their favorite pastimes was throwing darts, not at dartboards but at other kids. When I was four years old they had me running through passageways and dodging darts until Eddy, who was then fifteen years old, came to my rescue. He got in a couple of good licks, which gave me time to get away, but he paid a price. They pummeled him so thoroughly that he was black and blue for a week.

Mother had always been a very attractive woman. Not beautiful, but striking. She had a strong face, with high cheekbones, large eyes and full, dark brows, framed by a mane of deep brown hair. Every time I see a Joan Crawford movie I think of my mother. It is to Mother's credit that she maintained her good looks despite all she'd been through; living with an alcoholic while raising four kids couldn't have been easy on her. But there were added pressures. As Dad's condition worsened, he began drinking away his earnings; the support of the family fell on her shoulders.

Mother had worked before but never had her situation been so desperate; never had so many people depended upon her. She got a job in a small restaurant where she waited on tables, worked the counter and cash register. We lived off of her tips. Eventually, she was promoted to manager.

Mother was at work when Dad disappeared. I can't recall his leaving, only that he was there one day and gone the next. He left without saying a word to anyone. Not even a good-bye. It took a few days to sink in that he was really gone; we were so used to his not being around. Mother cried a little, God knows why. I guess after all they'd been through together she couldn't help but miss him. No one else did. From then on, for the next year anyway, it was just Mother, my brothers and sister, and I. Then an astounding thing happened; astounding only because it came as such a surprise. Mother began seeing another man. She wouldn't admit it, at first, but we knew. There were too many references to somebody named "Harold."

Mother dating? How did this person come into her life? She was home every evening and went to work every day. Where did they meet? Heavy stuff for a six-year-old to try and understand. William, Eddy and Ann couldn't come up with any answers either. The most logical explanation, on which they all agreed, was that mother had met Harold at the restaurant, where, over lingering cups of coffee, their relationship began to jell. Still, we didn't know for certain. And Mother wasn't talking.

One evening, Mother arrived home following an eight-hour shift, looking as fresh and relaxed - and, indeed, reborn - as if she really <u>was</u> Joan Crawford and had just come from makeup. She normally headed straight for bed, but this time was different. "Come on, kids, " she said, eagerly motioning us to her side. "Where do I begin?" she sighed, "How do I tell you about Harold?"

I had a feeling this was going to be big. I looked at my brothers and sister, but they were concentrating on mother, waiting to hear more.

"Let's see," she began slowly, "you remember hearing me mention Harold, don't you?" Heads nodded. "Well, he's a wonderful man, a very handsome man, as tall as Grandpa Barton but much bigger" - she held her hands out wide - "and so smart. He was a communications expert during the war and now he works for the telephone company. Harold has an excellent job and he makes good money. A lot of money, actually, but it hasn't spoiled him. He's very stable and sensible and down-to-earth. I know you'll like him very much."

"What does that mean?" William asked.

Mother smiled again, a coquettish smile I hadn't ever seen her display before. "Well, it means he's asked me to marry him," she said, pacing her words, "and I've accepted."

"Marry him?" Ann repeated.

"Yes, dear," Mother said. "I hope you're all happy for me."

"What about Daddy?" I piped up.

"You're father's gone," she answered quickly, her expression turning icy.

"But what if he comes back?"

"He won't be coming back because we're no longer married. I told you that, John, don't you remember?"

I didn't, not that it made any difference. At that age I wasn't quite clear about divorce, let alone marriage. As it turned out, Mother wasn't letting us in on her secret to gain our approval. It didn't matter that Eddy supported her, which he did, or that William disapproved, which he did, or that Ann and I were confused, which we were. Mother had already made up her mind to marry Harold. She did find a way of gaining our full backing, however, simply by telling us that Harold had promised to buy her a house in the country, and that we'd be leaving "The Project."

Harold kept his word. He bought a beautiful, white two-story frame house in a farming community midway between my grandparent's place and Columbus. It was one of the nicest homes in the area, and a big step up for Mother and her brood. Instead of being surrounded by brick and concrete, we had woods and creeks, open lands and clean, sweet-smelling air.

It didn't take us long to adjust to our new outdoor way of living. Mother and Ann started a huge garden - we had an acre to play with - planting flowers, fruit trees and endless rows of vegetables that would one day wind up as jams, jellies and relishes. My brothers taught me to hunt. The woods and fields were alive with rabbit, squirrel, pheasant and deer. I also learned how to set trap lines. In the wintertime, as I grew older, I set lines for mink, beaver and possum. I'd often wake up at 2:00 A.M. to clear the traps, skin the animals, salt and stretch the pelts before going to school. I'd run more lines in the afternoon on my way home.

My brothers and I caught so much game that Harold had to buy a freezer. It was a massive thing; so was the price tag that came with it. But Harold didn't complain. He was everything that Mother had described him to be - and a little bit more. It was the "extras" that caused Harold's stock to nose-dive in everyone's eyes but Mother's. Harold had misrepresented his finances. Either he wasn't as well off as he'd claimed to be or he'd over extended himself with the move to the country, or both. One thing was certain, his income fell short of what he needed to pay off the big house and support a large, ready-made family. As a consequence, we were forced to fend for ourselves whenever we needed anything.

"If you need new school clothes, or whatever," Mother would mutter repeatedly, sounding like a tape recorded message, "then go out and earn them."

By the time Harold's finances became a real concern, I was an old hand at running trap lines. The money I made from selling pelts came in handy but it never seemed to add up fast enough. So, between chores around the house and my schoolwork, I baled hay, collected maple syrup, and shoveled snow, depending on the season. For food, the family relied almost entirely on Mother's garden and hunting. I'd learned to hunt as a sport, then had to turn to it for survival. Now, if anyone asks me to go hunting, I refuse. I do not approve of killing and maiming animals for sport. And I find it impossible to understand how anyone who calls himself a sportsman can stop at a McDonalds on the way to blowing off some poor animal's head.

Money, or the lack of it, was actually a minor problem in living with Harold; we'd managed on next to nothing before, thanks to Mother's tenacity and boundless determination. The real problem was Harold himself. He had a dark side, an ugly sickness that no one suspected until it was too late. The first indication that Harold was "different" became apparent several months after he and Mother married, when he began to have trouble getting out of bed in the mornings. Physically, he appeared fine, but he no longer greeted each day with his characteristic burst of energy. He turned suddenly depressed and listless, almost impossible to budge. Mother was understandably concerned, and baffled. "I don't know what to make of him," she would moan. "He seems to have lost interest in everything." Harold couldn't explain the change in his behavior either;

he didn't even try to make excuses. He simply moved about the house like a sloth as he readied for work.

He never missed a day on the job. Whatever possessed Harold didn't affect his performance at work. He functioned normally, his co-workers confided to Mother, offering a glimmer of encouragement. But they should have seen him at home. Night after night, he returned from the office and promptly fell asleep in his easy chair. When any of us called him to dinner, he waved us away. He even ignored Mother.

One evening, when everyone but Harold was seated for dinner, Mother announced that the meal had been served. Not getting a response, she called again. "Come, dear," she said, "your food's getting cold. We're waiting." Another moment of silence passed. "You must eat something, Harold," she pleaded. Once again, he failed to answer. This time Mother pushed herself from the table and made for the living room. She found Harold's chair empty. He had gone to bed.

Just when it appeared that Harold would never snap out of his lethargy, his condition completely reversed itself. For months, sleep had been his ally; now it became his enemy. He'd go for days without shutting his eyes. He turned unpredictable and often violent, even showing signs of madness. Harold didn't drink coffee or smoke anything, he wouldn't touch alcohol and he didn't take drugs. Nevertheless, he had all the symptoms of the worst junkie imaginable. Deprived of drugs, an addict will try to run over his best friend with a car, beat him with a club, strangle cats and kill dogs. Harold was not only capable of doing those things, he did them. Once he even rammed his hand through a harvesting machine, cutting off his thumb and three of his fingers. When he woke up from surgery, he told mother, "I'll never have to work again." Harold was always gentle with Mother. He never raised a hand to her, but he sure beat the shit out of her kids. My older brothers and sister got the worst of it until they became of age and moved out, unable to take his abuse anymore. That left me as the only target around.

One day, Harold kicked me in the spine when I failed to respond to his order to take out the trash. "I shouted your name ten times," he roared. "John! John! John! Your name's John, isn't it?"

"I guess I didn't hear you, Harold," I said earnestly. "I'm sorry..." Wham!

Another time he threw me down a flight of twelve stairs to the concrete floor of the basement. I had my head rammed into heavy oak doors more times than I care to remember. I got slugged in the face and knocked over backward, then picked up by the ankles and spanked while airborne. If he was really angry he turned me around and slammed a fist into my stomach.

It's unfair to say that Harold had turned completely mad. For the first few years, he was up and down, alternating between manic-depressive states. We loved him when he was down because he was so harmless; he never even talked. But with the turnabout he became a horror. We could sense the switch coming. Watching Harold was like watching an animal before an earthquake. He grew restless and acted in a manner that was abnormal, even for him. Eventually, we were able to mark his changes by the calendar, as he'd go through exact six-month cycles.

When I was nine, Mother gave birth to another son, David, and from that day on my life at home was never the same. As Harold's flesh and blood, David could do no wrong. Anything David wanted was his, even if it didn't belong to him. To make certain that David always got his way, Harold taught him to scream at the top of his powerful little lungs, which brought Harold running. David was never satisfied with his own toys. He wanted what belonged to me, things I had bought with my hard-earned money. David wound up with them and I was left with bruises.

"Why is Harold always hitting me?" I asked Mother one day as she pressed a cold cloth against my reddened cheek.

"He doesn't mean to, sweetheart. It's just that he can't help himself. "

"Then why doesn't he hit David? David can do anything and I get the blame."

"David's just a baby," she replied, "he doesn't know what he's doing."

"Yes, he does."

"Let's not make trouble, darling. Let's try to be nice to David, and Harold too. Harold needs all our help and prayers."

Pray for Harold? Be nice to Harold? I couldn't do that. It was much easier to hide whenever Harold was around. The dining room provided the perfect hideaway. We had a huge dining table, made of oak, that Mother always kept extended with three large leaves and covered with a heavy damask cloth that reached to the floor. The table was seldom used, except for holidays and the rare times we had company. We always ate in the kitchen. Every time I'd hear Harold's car pulling into the driveway, I'd run for cover under the table. Some of my fondest memories are of listening to the family fighting, going crazy, while I lay peacefully on my back staring at its underside. Resurfacing, without being seen, took some planning. I always tried to wait until dinner time, when everyone was seated in the kitchen. At that point, Harold would inevitable bellow, "Where the fuck is that kid!" With that I'd appear as if I'd just come in from playing outside. My luck held out for nearly two years. Then one day, for some reason, Harold looked under the table. I knew I was in trouble even before his big paw shot forward. "Damn you," he roared, "I've been calling for ten minutes!" I felt myself being dragged out into the open by the seat of my pants, and the pounding began.

On Sunday mornings, I sought refuge in church. Harold attended church too - he came from a strict religious family, Mother said - so I lingered long after the services for Sunday school. That went on for nearly twelve years. For my perfect attendance, I later received a certificate.

I discovered the town library as well. It was small and

quiet and private, seldom occupied by more than five people at once. Following the dining room table incident, I spent most of my time secluded between rows of bookshelves. I became an avid reader. Historical novels interested me most, and anything that had to do with nature and ancient civilizations. To me, the real mysteries were not by Agatha Christie and Erle Stanley Gardner but why archaeologists explored the ruins of lost cultures.

"Where have you been all day, John?" someone in the family would ask when I returned home.

"Walking in the woods," I'd reply. Or "hunting." I didn't dare tell the truth. The library had become my secret hiding place where I could weave fantasies without their interference. The first really happy time in my life, thinking back, was spent sitting by myself reading a stack of books.

The library happened to be located in what was known as Town Hall. The police department and jail were in the basement; on the top floor were administrative and mayor's offices. The rest of the building housed the local movie theater. That was another good place to escape, when it was open (one day a week) and I could afford the price of admission. We didn't get too many big movies, mainly old Westerns and serials with Lash LaRue, Hopalong Cassidy, Gene Autry and Roy Rogers. I especially liked the way Lash LaRue brought the bad guys to their knees with his whip. I wanted one like it to beat the shit out of Harold.

The really good movies played in Columbus, but that didn't stop me. I'd hop a bus and I was on my way to the big city. With John Wayne or Spencer Tracy waiting at the other end, I would have trekked almost anywhere. I often saw their films two and three times, if not in one sitting then on successive weekends.

Not all of the movies that passed through town were wholesome and clean; some never even made it to Columbus. I'd recently turned twelve when I heard about a foreign film that was causing quite a furor across the country. The movie starred a young French actress, Brigitte Bardot, and from its title, <u>And God Created Woman</u>, it sounded rather pious. According to the paper, it definitely wasn't. There were scenes where Bardot, who was fast becoming known as a "sex kitten," bared her breasts while portraying a pouting child-women who openly advocated freedom of choice in sexual partners.

Members of our town council insisted on screening the film prior to scheduling it for showing in the local theater, a practice they followed with every film. How else could they uphold the strict moral standards of the community? Silently, the council members probably enjoyed Bardot and her shameless sexual appetite (on film, anyway), but being responsible men, they blackballed the movie. The fuss they created in judging the film "dirty" undoubtedly left more of an impression on me than if I'd seen it.

Sex was not a subject to be discussed openly. The slightest reference to anything sexual at a mixed gathering brought gasps and glares from the women present, and a certain reprisal for the offending party later on. No one fondled in public; few people touched. Men told "shady" stories and talked of lustful escapades in private or in small groups at neighborhood taverns. Boys gathered in hidden places, like behind barns, to exchange secrets meant only for young ears. As kids growing up in farm country, we all knew what was going on. We'd have had to wear blinders not to know. Everywhere we looked, animals were fornicating, constantly and without inhibition. Watching them became a natural part of our lives. My first sexual experience occurred when I was eight years old. I'd fooled around some before that, playing "stinky finger" with one of the little neighbor girls, but nothing more serious than "let me touch yours and I'll let you touch mine." She touched - at times stroking my "thing" as if it were a pet snake - and I probed. We both giggled.

There were no laughs with Gloria. Every once in a while Mother and Harold liked to go into town at night. Mother hesitated leaving me alone after dark (my brothers and Ann were never home), so she lined up a baby sitter. Young girls who'd work for nothing weren't easy to find, but Gloria didn't mind. A few jars of Mother's homemade preserves would be payment enough, thank you.

Gloria was a high school sophomore and very pretty, although slightly on the chunky side. She wore tight sweaters and skirts, which tended to make her appear heavier than she really was. "I've found a new diet," she'd tell me each time she came to visit. "Do you think it's doing any good?" Then she'd stand before a mirror, suck in her stomach, and rub her hands along her ample hips, thighs and breasts.

One night, Gloria put me to bed and went directly into the adjoining bathroom, leaving the door partially open. I didn't think anything about it; in fact, I tried to sleep, but Gloria had other plans for me. It wasn't the light that bothered me, or the sound of water running into the wash basin. It was Gloria herself. Gloria in action. From my bed I could see not only Gloria's reflection in one of the full-length bathroom mirrors, but also Gloria peeling off her clothes. She liked to disrobe and admire herself. She was good at it, too. She performed one of the most erotic stripteases I've ever seen. The only thing missing was bump-and-grind music.

Standing before the mirror, as if in a spotlight, she unbuttoned her blouse and slowly let it fall from her shoulders to the floor. Then she unhooked her bra, shaking the straps loose one by one until her huge breasts were fully exposed. Unzipping her skirt, she stepped out of it and pulled down her panties. Fully naked, she stood basking in her own reflection, caressing her body with smooth, tender strokes. Except for the photos in the nudist magazine, which I hardly remembered, I'd never seen a woman naked before. I knew I liked it.

Gloria could see me in the mirror just as I could see her. I pretended to be asleep, but she wasn't fooled; she knew I wasn't lying under a tent pole. It pleased her to know that her body excited me, even though I wouldn't let on. "What do you think you're looking at?" she shrieked, as if suddenly stunned to discover she was being watched. She held a towel primly against her breasts, even though she knew full well that I could see her exposed backside in the mirror. "I know what you're thinking, you bad boy!"

I was certain that God would strike me dead!

Once Gloria had her say she returned to the mirror for more self-examination and adoring caresses. When she tired of that, she moved to the bathroom sink, filled it with warm water, and began washing herself with a dampened cloth. This process took a good half-hour, most of which was spent on her breasts. Gloria worshipped her breasts, and they were magnificent, large and firm with dollar-sized pink disks surrounding the nipples. She washed over them, and around them, and under them, then repeated the cycle before moving down her stomach and between her legs. Finished at last, she disappeared momentarily. The next thing I knew she as standing over me wearing only a towel, sarong-style. "Did you take a bath before you went to bed?" she barked. I had, but I didn't want her to know. More than anything, I wanted to get in the bathroom with her.

"No," I fibbed.

"Well, you have to take one," she ordered. Gloria marched out of the room and started filling the tub. I followed, in my underwear, and watched as the water began to rise. She squirted something under the faucet that brought forth a wave of bubbles. "OK, get in," she said, "and make sure you wash everything."

As I pulled off my underwear and stepped into the foamy tub, Gloria returned to the basin, dropped her towel, and began cleansing herself all over again. With her back to me, my view was obstructed, but from the position of her hands I could tell she was working around her genitalia.

"What are you staring at?" she snapped, looking over her shoulder.

"Nothing," I gulped.

She glared momentarily before darting toward me to grab my ear. Tugging at it, she said angrily, "Don't you ever wash these things?" Without waiting for an answer, she took the wash rag, the one she'd been using on herself, soaped it and stuck it in my ear - hard. (Gloria had the strength of a bull.) I started to yell, but she ran the soapy rag across my mouth, muffling my cries. "Now for the rest of you," she said.

She lathered my head, then dunked it underwater. Then she ran the cloth down my back and around my buttocks, lingering around the cleavage, fingering it deeply. Her breasts grazed my arm. The nipples were swollen and taut. "Stand up," she barked.

I hesitated. I was not in any condition to stand; part of me was already up, anyway.

"Get on your feet!" Gloria said, with a strange look on her face. As she grabbed under my arms and pulled me out of the water, her eyes suddenly grew wide. "What's <u>that</u> for?" she asked, stepping back a bit to get a better view of my stiffened appendage.

"I don't know," I said, naively.

Gloria looked at me savagely. "You play with yourself, don't you?"

"No, I answered emphatically. "That's a sin."

"Have you ever touched a girl before?"

"No," I said, discounting my earlier "stinky finger" experience. She looked at me sternly while soaping her hand, then wrapping it around the hardened rod.

Then she began stroking it. I had my first orgasm that night.

As Gloria was tucking me back in bed, she asked, "Are you going to tell you mother I gave you a bath?"

"No," I replied, definitely.

"Did you like the bath I gave you?"

"Yes."

"Well then, whenever you have to have a babysitter, make sure you ask for me."

"I will," I replied. I had no say in the matter, but I promised anyway.

"And never tell anybody what we did. Swear?"

"I swear."

A few months later, shortly after my ninth birthday, I discovered what it was really like to be with a girl. Mary Kay was the daughter of a neighbor, and we often walked to school together. I had not seen her in weeks, but we met one hot, steamy afternoon on a country road. She was wearing a little cotton sun dress, and she looked terrific. "Want to take a walk?" I asked. "We could let our feet dangle in the creek."

She brushed a wisp of blond hair out of her face and smiled. "Sure, that would feel good." We made it as far as the bridge that crossed the creek; actually, into the cool shadows beneath the bridge. There, nothing grew except the softest, greenest moss; it felt like a carpet of velour under our bare feet. I had known Mary Kay ever since we'd moved to the country. She was a good friend, nothing more. But suddenly I felt a stirring between my legs. I turned on my side to face her as she lay on her stomach, and ran my hand along the gentle curve of her back. Her body quivered, and she rolled over. I placed my hand on her stomach, making broad, sweeping, circular motions until my fingers rested in the damp folds between her thighs. I'd never played "stinky finger" with Mary Kay before, and she did not seem to mind my starting now, although she kept her legs firmly together. I was leaning over to kiss her cheek when she came up with the oddest remark. Looking up, she said, "I was watching my sister kiss her boyfriend the other night and they were sticking their tongues in each other's mouths."

"You mean, she stuck her tongue in <u>his</u> mouth?"

"No, he stuck his tongue in <u>her</u> mouth." I looked at

Mary Kay and made a face.

"Why?" I asked.

"I don't know," she shrugged, "but want to see what it feels like?" I wasn't quite sure, but I nodded anyway. To kiss, seriously, we had to get close, and when we did my penis brushed against the softness of her leg. The feel of her body against mine brought on a feeling I'd never known before, and I thought: There cannot be anything better in this world than being this close to another human being.

Mary Kay pressed her lips mine and we touched tongues. It felt slimy and I backed away. "No," she said, "you're supposed to suck on my tongue."

"Are you sure?"

"Yes," she said, impatiently.

Again, we kissed and once again I felt her tongue in my mouth. "That's awful," I said, wiping my open mouth with the back of my hand.

"No, it isn't! It's OK - my sister does it."

My interest in Mary Kay was slowly fading, but I didn't want her mad at me. "All right," I said, "We'll do it."

At that point, I noticed a strange thing happening. As I worked on Mary Kay's tongue, she began to spread her legs - like the unfolding of flower petals. Now my fingers could freely explore the soft, resilient flesh of her uncharted depths. Then I felt her hand. She had a death grip on my rod. "You're squeezing too hard," I said. It felt dead, but I still had an erection.

"Well, how do you want me to touch it?"

"Just hold it, "I said," but not so tight."

"I saw my brother play with himself once," Mary Kay whispered, "so I know how boys do it." She loosened her grip slightly and began moving her hand slowly up and down. After only a few strokes, she stopped. Her eyes grew wide as she said, "I know an even better way. Want to try?"

"What do you mean?"

Mary Kay pushed my probing fingers away and spread her legs farther apart, lifting her knees into the air. "Closer," she coaxed, "move closer."

She pointed the object in her hand, guiding me inside. Then I was on top of her. And we kissed - with our tongues. I thought I'd gone to Heaven.

Our bodies locked tightly together for several moments, squirming unexpectedly at the wild and totally new sensation that gripped us. Then, suddenly and without warning, Mary Kay shoved me away. She was on her feet in an instant, reaching for her panties and sun dress, and climbing quickly into them, tugging awkwardly at the skimpy pieces in an almost desperate attempt to cover herself. She dressed with her back to me, without saying a word, and without so much as a parting glance she hastily departed the shadowy "scene of the crime" for the open spaces and sunlight.

Mary Kay's quick departure didn't bother me. In fact, I felt relieved to have her break away, and grateful for her silence. Had she said anything, even in passing, I probably wouldn't have answered; my mind was too filled with ugly, horrifying thoughts. The overwhelming joy that had raced through me at the height of our intimacy had turned to fear and shame. It was as if a dense, black cloud had rolled over me, smothering me with guilt. I had tasted Heaven. Now I was certain the Devil had taken me by the hand and was leading me straight to Hell. It was difficult for me to understand how something that felt so good could be considered so wrong, even evil. I needed desperately to talk to someone, anyone, but that was impossible. I couldn't confide in my brothers or sister, and certainly not in my Mother or Harold. We were not allowed to think about sex, let alone discuss it. To admit that I had actually <u>experienced</u> sex would have been intolerable.

My feelings toward Mary Kay swayed from one extreme to the other. One moment, I wanted to see her again to try and make peace with her, and myself; the next moment, I blamed her for causing me so much pain, and pledged never to even mention her name. If it hadn't been for that afternoon under the bridge, I kept telling myself, we'd still be best friends. Instead, we had become strangers. My guilt was so complete that I began to doubt whether I'd ever look at another girl. (I was certain I'd never <u>touch</u> one.) But, for reasons that were unknown to me at the time, whenever I thought of Mary Kay, which was almost constantly, I'd relive our few moments of innocent discovery and my body would throb with sexual tension. Once again, I'd be lifted sky-high with pleasure, only to come crashing down in despair that lingered long after the all-too-fleeting pleasure.

How could I ever be forgiven my sin? To my young mind, I had committed the greatest sin of all; one twenty times more deadly than masturbation. Mostly, I wanted to avoid Mary Kay. That was easy for a time, especially on weekdays. Because of summer vacation, there were no morning walks together to school, no sitting within glancing distance of each other in the same classroom.

Once school started in the fall, I purposely left the house earlier than necessary so that our paths would not cross. For safe measure, I took short cuts, racing through the woods, across cornfields and meadows. In the classroom, Mary Kay sat behind me, several rows away. By getting to my seat first, and leaving last, I could go for days without seeing her.

Sundays were a horror, as our families made it a ritual to attend church together. There were so many of us that we usually took two cars, but Mary Kay and I, whom our well-meaning mothers regarded as "the two chums," were often paired. That meant riding with her to church in the same car, sliding into the same pew next to her, and joining her in the fun and games between services and Sunday school. The only time we spoke was on the playground, where Mary Kay liked to ride the swings. Before the incident under the bridge, she didn't mind where I'd put my hands to shove her back and forth. I liked pushing on her soft bottom rather than her trim, little waist, and so did she. Then it was harmless; now it was dirty. "Don't you dare touch me!" she cried, setting the rules for months to come.

"I won't, don't worry," I replied. From then on I was careful to make contact only with the swingboard.

Sunday was the day the smothering black cloud was at its worst, and it wasn't all due to Mary Kay's presence. Listening to the minister had a devastating effect on me. For some reason, his sermons always focused on sex, or some aspect of it. He preached about lust, and condemned people who "go' a whoring" and commit "whoredom." He talked endlessly (or so it seemed) about wickedness and nakedness and immorality. I heard about incest and adultery, of men who "waste their seeds," and of wicked, sinful places like Sodom and Gomorrah. Every time he opened his mouth I squirmed in my seat. When he gestured with his hands, as he often did, his finger seemed to point directly at me. It didn't, really - but it took me many years to figure that out. His sermons were pure vaudeville, and he was playing to his audience. Where else could the people of this little farming community hear sex discussed openly (it was the only x-rated show in town), and with the blessing of the church? Topics considered "forbidden" not only kept the parishioners awake, but also had them returning every Sunday and filling the collection plate to overflowing.

The passing months did little to ease my conscience, or dim my memories of that steamy afternoon with Mary Kay. Winters in the Ohio Valley can be fierce, raw and blustery. But no matter how numbing the cold, thoughts of our time together never failed to generate heat between my legs. One freezing January day, as I was returning from setting trap lines in the snow-covered woods, I spotted Mary Kay walking along the road. She was bundled from head to toe, but the sight of her fascinated me. I crouched low, not wanting her to see me, then began following her, careful to keep a safe distance between us. She turned into her driveway, bypassed her house, then disappeared inside the barn-like, tool shed in the back yard. I couldn't imagine what she was doing in there, and I really didn't care - but I suddenly found myself at the shed door, pushing it open. Mary Kay was sitting on an old crate, huddled next to a frost-caked window. She turned away from me and said, "What are you doing here?"

"I don't know," I replied, closing the door.

"Well, you'd better go."

"I want to stay," I said, stubbornly. The admission surprised me. Until that moment, I hadn't realized how much I wanted to be with her.

"Well, you can't."

"Why?"

"You can't, that's all. Just leave me alone."

I moved closer to Mary Kay, stepping cautiously over scattered nails and bits of broken wood. "You haven't really spoken to me since we were underneath the bridge."

She raised a mittened hand to the frosty pane and ran her fingers in small circles, creating a blurred pattern. "You haven't spoken to me either," she said, finally.

"I've thought about it."

"I'm glad you didn't," she sighed, her breath clearly visible in the cold air. "We're not supposed to talk to each other."

"Why? Who said that? Did you tell your mother?"

She turned slowly to look at me. Her face, the small portion that peeked through the furry trim on the hood of her parka, showed no sign of anger. "No, I didn't tell anyone," she answered, calmly, "but what we did was wrong."

"I think it was wrong, too."

"You do?" she said quickly. She actually sounded relieved that we were talking.

"Yes - and I don't think we should ever do it again."

Mary Kay sighed once more, sending a shaft of white air across my cheeks. "I don't either," she agreed.

I smiled and so did she. Then I sat beside her and we talked about our guilt, and unhappiness, and all the things we'd missed by avoiding each other the past months. We were completely open and honest, especially about sex. Somehow, the subject always came back to that. "Being with you was one of the best things that's ever happened to me," I admitted. "Except for Christmas mornings, nothing has ever made me feel so good." Looking into Mary Kay's eyes, I knew I wanted to feel good again. The pleasure she gave me, no matter how fleeting, made all the guilt seem worthwhile.

My hand found its way to Mary Kay's thigh, and I began stroking it very gently. A moment later we were standing, unzipping our jeans, and pressing our warm bodies together. We didn't even notice the icy cold that surrounded us.

I saw Mary Kay many times after that.

And Gloria.

There were other young girls as well.

In the four years since I began straying to escape Harold's tirades, I learned that home was not the place for me. Home stood for pain and violence, fighting and bickering, anger and hiding out. In its place, I discovered a worthy substitute in sex. Sex brought a closeness of one on one. It allowed me to be warm and caring, to kiss and touch, to experience pleasure. It was, I felt, the perfect intimacy between the love and feeling that I should have been receiving at home. As such, any strange girl became more family to me than my own family.

As I entered my teen years, I turned more and more to sex. It was the only "family" I needed. I knew, too, that I had just about all of Harold that I could take for one lifetime. I needed to get away, but I wasn't exactly sure how to go about that. My young mind finally came up with a plan, and that was to join the army. There was only one hitch. Because of my age, I needed the approval of a parent. My mother didn't argue. She signed the papers and I was gone.

Believe it or not, the army was good for me. I can't honestly say that it taught me any morals or sense of responsibility; I had been raised with those qualities. I can't even say that it taught me to be an excellent sharp shooter since hunting in the woods all those years had made me a "good shot." But I did learn something and it wasn't in any manual. What the army taught me was that there was a whole world of sex I had yet to discover.

While stationed in Germany, I heard about a cathouse filled with voluptuous women of various ages and sizes. But just hearing about it wasn't good enough for me; I had to check it out for myself. It didn't take long for the madam, a woman edging into her forties, to learn of my "talent," and once she did she refused to allow any of her girls to be alone with me. I was hers and that was final; she made that clear to everyone under her roof. Being the young man that I was, I didn't argue considering the nature of the place. Besides, I didn't have to pay for any of the services as the other customers did. It was a great arrangement

Whenever I had a night off or a weekend pass, just about everyone at the base knew where to find me because I was always with Madam Helga. Everything was going smoothly until one day I arrived to find Madam Helga away on an errand. A lot of the girls flirted with me whenever they had the chance, but few of them would cross the line for fear of losing not only their jobs but also their nightly romps with horny soldiers. But with Madam Helga gone, one hot little number decided the risk was hers for the taking and, under the circumstance, I wasn't about to argue. We were going at it hot and heavy when Madam Helga suddenly burst into the room. That's when I learned the meaning of the words, "Hell hath no fury like a woman scorned." Ranting and raving, Madam Helga dragged my lusty partner-of-the-moment out of bed and down the stairs by her golden hair, then out the door, all the while threatening that she would end up in a box if she ever returned. By the time Madam Helga came back for me, I too was gone, never to return to her establishment again. That confrontation left a lasting impression on my young mind for it was the first time I really ever experienced the wrath of jealousy. I guess I didn't expect "an older woman" to react that way.

While in the army I met Tony. He was from New York City and he seemed to know all the ropes when it came to seducing women, sometimes for lust, sometimes to boost his ego, but more than anything, for money. Tony fascinated me with stories of his sexual escapades and, before long, I found myself hanging around the young dark-haired fellow with the piercing blue eyes. How he could end up with the most gorgeous girls, then later brag about the money and jewels they would insist he have, absolutely amazed me. He had so many girls in love with him at one time that he could have given some young movie star stud a run for his money. I liked women, too, and I loved to have sex, but Tony gave a whole different meaning to "enjoying a job well done."

Tony and I were released from the army together on August 24, 1964, sixteen days after my twentieth birthday. During our time together in Germany, Tony had invited me to go to Brooklyn with him to check out the sights before my return to Ohio. I wasn't in a hurry to get back there anyway, and I hadn't a clue of what I was supposed to do with my life. "Why not?" I told him.

Tony became a very good friend, and a very good teacher. He introduced me to so many people in the fast lane I thought my head would never stop spinning. Why, there were more women in New York than there were farmhouses in Ohio! I thought I had been a sex-craved fiend before I returned to the states, now I knew I was for sure.

The sexual revolution was clearly on its way in New York. I realized that once I had gone out with the sister of one of

Tony's girlfriends. At first she came off as being a petite, seemingly shy little gal, but she ended up being a flying nymph. Shy? I don't think so.

The next day Tony approached me with an odd look on his face. Apparently my date told her sister of my unusual appendage, who was then on the phone to tell Tony. I was really embarrassed when he asked me if it was true that I had three legs? (Tony had seen me naked but never with a hard on.) My embarrassment soon faded, however, when he began to tell me how much money I could make with my "extra leg." That was all it took to wet my appetite, and before I could change my mind, Tony was teaching me the fine art of being a male prostitute.

It wasn't long before I was having more fun than I'd ever had in my life. Who would have thought that little (big) "Johnny Buck" from Ohio could have his cake and eat enough of it to survive in New York City? A definite improvement from the life I thought I'd be returning to, without question. For seven months, I had all the sex I could handle, my pockets were always filled with money, car keys, jewelry, and all the night life I could handle. But I was living a fantasy that seemed to be spinning out of control. Satisfying as it was, I knew I couldn't go on like that much longer without burning out - or getting in deep trouble. There was something else. Strange as it seems, I had been raised with strong morals, and a voice within me kept saying, "This is really crazy."

I had heard about the warm paradise-like climate on the California coast. All the babes in their little bikinis soaking up the sun would be more welcome than the brutal cold I had grown so tired of. I could get a job, go to school and learn all about Hollywood. I halfheartedly joked around with myself saying, "Who knows, I might even be in a movie someday." I never really believed that would happen of course, but the warm, sunny climate, and the beaches filled with shapely women, were enticement enough for me to seek the journey.

It wasn't much later that I bought a bus ticket and headed west, first stopping to see my family. (I had hoped to avoid Harold but I knew if I wanted to be with everyone else I'd run into his sorry ass.) I even visited Mary Kay while I was there. She was going through some really hard times and needed money desperately. I gave her all the cash I had but twenty dollars, figuring she needed it more than I did. I was certain I could get more where that came from. Maybe I felt guilty about the way I made the money and believed that helping Mary Kay would right what was wrong. All I know is that helping her made me feel better.

After my short stay in Ohio I was without enough money for a bus ticket that would take me all the way to California. I went as far as I could on fifteen dollars then started hitch-hiking westward across the states. From then on it was odd jobs along the way, whatever it took to get across the miles.

CHAPTER 3

I thought I'd never get to California. I wasn't in any rush; still, there were times when I thought I'd never get out of Missouri. With no money, it seemed I was stopping at every farmhouse along the way to ask for a day or two of work, a meal and a place to sleep in the barn. "I just got out of the military," I'd tell the farmers, "and all my money's been stolen. I am trying to get home to California." A blatant lie, but I had to earn some cash. Half the time I got lucky. A few good people even gave me five or ten dollar handouts as I was on my way again.

The pace picked up once I crossed the Oklahoma State line. As I was hitchhiking along the highway, a man in a new Mustang stopped to give me a ride. His name was Terry and he had recently left his wife in Virginia to head for Hollywood to try for a career in acting. When I heard where he was going I knew my days of roughing it were over. Unfortunately, Terry was also short of cash. By the time we reached Texas, both of us were stone-broke. This time I took the easy way out. A collect call to my mother netted us twenty bucks, enough to get us to California. We looked like a million dollars traveling in Terry's new car, but we were counting our pennies the rest of the way.

I was hoping that Terry and I could share a room or small apartment once we arrived in Hollywood. He was an easygoing, pleasant guy in his mid-twenties; we got along great together, no problems. But Terry had other plans. "I'll be staying with friends in the San Fernando Valley," he told me. "You're welcome to come along. It's a big house. They have plenty of room." I thought I was doing the right thing by turning down his offer. Once Terry had driven away, however, I found myself stranded in a strange city with no place to go, and without money.

Hollywood in March 1965, was even more bustling than it is today. The streets were crowded not only with tourists eager to see all the sights, but with people who worked at the networks - CBS and ABC - as well as the local radio and television stations, and nearby motion picture and recording studios. Then there were the movie and legitimate theaters with their glittering marquees, the restaurants and night spots, and the shiny stars of the Walk of Fame. Wandering about was fun for a time, but I felt totally lost.

I had one phone number in my pocket. It belonged to a family in Garden Grove, former neighbors from back home in Ohio. Where Garden Grove was exactly, I had no idea, but it sounded nice and it was in Southern California. As it turned out, Garden Grove wasn't too far away, southeast of Los Angeles near Anaheim, the home of Disneyland. With an invitation to stay with our ex-neighbors, I found myself on the road again, hitchhiking to Garden Grove.

The family couldn't have been nicer to "Johnny." For next to nothing, I was put up in a small but private room with connecting bath, given kitchen privileges and a key to come and go as I pleased. Within a few days I landed a job as an ambulance driver, which had me cramming the Thomas Guide every night to learn where the hell I was going at full speed with siren wailing and lights flashing. I knew from the start I wouldn't last long. If there's one thing that really gets to me it's seeing someone or something suffer - people, animals, anything. In the weeks that I stayed with the Ambulance Company I saw more gore than I thought I'd ever see again. Freeway accidents, hit-and-runs on city streets, twisted, beat-up bodies in their homes. Kids, grown-ups, elderly people. To get up every morning and know that I would have to face that at least once during the day was more than I could handle. So I quit and began a series of odd jobs that took me from a candy factory to selling furniture, then shoes, the Fuller brushes door to door. None of these jobs lasted long either, nor did they interest me. More than anything I wanted to study cinematography at UCLA.

By June I was back in Hollywood, this time sleeping next to a trash can behind the Cave Theatre at night and washing dishes at a hot dog stand on Hollywood Boulevard by day. I could have rented a cheap flophouse room somewhere, I suppose, but I was trying to save, not spend. I can be a real hoarder with money, especially when I have a goal in mind.

It was over the counter at the hot dog stand that I met Linda. A regular lunchtime customer, she worked within walking distance at a law office as a secretary. Within the week, Linda had a new roommate.

Living with Linda in her apartment was the best thing that could have happened to me. It certainly had its advantages, sleeping with her for one. We had such good times in bed she rarely mentioned the rent money we had agreed to split. Even when she did mention money, it was with a wink.

On weekends Linda went her own way and I went mine, no questions asked. I welcomed the time to make extra money by washing cars, which meant my hands were in water seven days a week. I think I washed almost everything in Hollywood at that point. But I wasn't complaining for I finally had enough cash to enroll in the summer session at UCLA. To earn extra spending money, I applied for an on campus job as a nude model for Life Drawing classes. I did it as a lark really. With my string bean build, I knew I wasn't the model type. Still, I felt I had something of interest to offer the would-be Piccassos.

Linda was full of surprises too. One evening she arrived home from her office to tell me she'd had a fight with her boss and quit. I certainly wasn't making enough money to support the two of us until she found another position. But Linda had more to tell me, news that she'd been keeping to herself. Part of her job with the law firm had been to "entertain" the wealthy clientele. Suddenly everything began to add up. No wonder her weekends were always booked. No wonder she wasn't concerned about the rent money. She was raking it in on the side.

Linda didn't remain idle for long. She had enjoyed her extracurricular life so much at the law firm that she decided to make it her calling, and soon she was working the clubs along the Sunset Strip. With Linda away nights and sleeping days, I was offered her car whenever I needed it. The only thing missing in our busy lives was a campus-parking permit for me.

It was at that point that I arrived back at the apartment to be confronted with Linda's intriguing proposal. "How would you like to make a hundred bucks?" she wanted to know. All I had to do was screw her while a camera recorded the action for a stag film.

Hell, I wasn't going into politics or planning on becoming famous. I just wanted to get my hands on some fast parking permit money. As it turned out, performing with Linda was the easiest money I had ever made, and I didn't have to get my hands wet. Within an hour Harry had peeled the silver foil from the window, dismantled the lights, packed up his Super 8mm camera and, with a slobbering grin, handed me a check for one hundred dollars. I was smiling, too, until I discovered the check was no good.

CHAPTER 4

L ittle did I realize that the onetime gig with Harry would land me a career. I did know one thing for certain, however. If I were to continue performing in Harry's kind of filmmaking, cash was the only way to go. No more bounced checks for me! From that day on I began telling people that my middle initial "C," stood for *cash.* I never liked my real middle name, anyway.

My experience with Harry convinced me there was money to be made in modeling. The thought so consumed me that I began looking through classified ads in the *L.A. Free Press* in the hope of finding leads for part-time jobs to fit into my class schedule. Most of the listings were come-ons from characters that wanted up front money themselves. "Give us fifty bucks," they told me, "and we'll take photos for your portfolio." It was the people who didn't ask for handouts that caught my attention. As it turned out, they were looking for nude models.

I began showing up at Crossroads of the World, an attractive Hollywood landmark, of sorts, on Sunset Boulevard. Behind the storefront facades, in darkened back rooms, were miniature sound stages. Nothing fancy, just a few lights on tripods, a camera, scattered pieces of worn furniture, a rumpled bed and backdrops. It wasn't MGM, but something obviously was happening between the walls. Unknowingly, I had stumbled onto the pornography capital of the United States.

My first assignments were for magazine work. In the mid-1960s, a male model had to keep his back to the camera. I even had to keep my underwear on since showing a man's ass was illegal - or so they told me. Then they began to get really chancy and off came the underwear. For a series of shots, I had to dry hump a girl model. Everything was simulated but it looked real in the photo. Probably too real for once the shots got into circulation, the photographer got busted. But times were changing. The court decided the photos were not obscene, which led to frontal nudity and more. It was a gradual procedure until the courts allowed even penetration to be shown.

Each of the shops at Crossroads had a porno shooter who shot everything from nude stills to live action 8mm "loops." I remember walking into one shop shortly after my first visit to meet a photographer named Dave who had taken stills of two girls in a lesbian scene with a black guy. Dave was scared stiff. He had just received a phone call to alert him that he was in trouble. Without another word Dave was loading all his negatives and camera equipment into his Cadillac and speeding away down Sunset. Not thirty seconds later, what appeared to be the entire L.A.P.D. Vice Squad swarmed Dave's studio. He had gotten away just in time.

Sex was all around me. I was drawn to it and it was drawn to me. The producers, if they could be called that, were anxious to get me away from posing for magazine shots and into film work. What made me valuable, they said, was my size, my ability to sustain an erection, and orgasm on cue.

With film offers suddenly coming my way, I dropped out of UCLA. For the first time in my life I was making decent money, and I had found something I really liked doing. It was certainly more enjoyable, for me anyway, than washing dishes, selling brushes and chasing accidents. I was also getting an education in cinematography without having to pay for it. When I wasn't performing, I visited other filming sessions at Crossroads where I learned camera techniques from the cameramen, lighting, makeup and various ways to dress a set. It was all small-time, bottom level, but it was a start. Actually, a few of the men were quite knowledgeable about filmmaking. At one session, a cameraman who had worked for Cecil B. DeMille during the early days of talkies befriended me. Meeting him gave me the feeling that I was headed in the right direction, despite the surroundings.

The movies being made at Crossroads were no different than the movie Harry made of Linda and me at our apartment that night. By today's standards they weren't really movies at all, but rather minutes-long "loops," short scenes of quickie sex action that have been shown for years at adult arcades for a quarter a throw. Loops had no real story lines, no sound, and were shot in black and white. Quick to make and easy money.

Loops were hot stuff in those days. Shot on Super-8 film, they were reduced to 8mm and packaged in plain white boxes, which were delivered to an underground lab. There, five hundred to one thousand copies were made and the negatives destroyed. Today, loops would be pushed as "limited editions," but at that time they were totally illegal and had to be sold undercover, usually out of the trunks of cars parked near magazine stands, bookstores, even bars.

In the mid-1960s, a loop sold for fifty dollars. Even a minimum sale of five hundred loops brought in big bucks. The only out-of-pocket expenses were for lab cost and the models. It was even more profitable when the models were given bum checks.

During that time it seemed everything was starting to come my way. I had plenty of job offers, sex (on and off the set), and the money was getting better and better. The only thing I didn't have in my life was stability. But I was hoping to fill that void, too. I had met a girl months earlier when I had worked for the Ambulance Company. Her name was Sharon. She was a nurse at County-USC Medical Center where she worked on a team that was pioneering open-heart surgery.

Sharon and I had hit it off together almost from the start. I began calling her again, then seeing her, and things got serious. I wanted to keep them that way so I never mentioned what I was doing for a living. It wasn't that I was embarrassed, I simply wanted everything to be perfect. Above all, I didn't want to lose her. It worked out fine that way. Sharon and I were married in the fall of 1965.

I should have been honest with her because when I did admit to what I was doing, her reaction was exactly as I feared it would be. I can hear her voice now as she said, darkly, "You're having sex with other women?"

I told her they meant nothing to me; I had absolutely no feeling for those women. I was simply doing a job, my job. That was the way I made money. It would take a special person to understand what I was saying. Sharon was special in many ways. She was bright, attractive, levelheaded, stable. But she could not accept my work.

Maybe I expected too much. Maybe *she* expected too much. I only know that from that point on our marriage was over. And while we remained married for the next nineteen years, we lived together for only a handful of them and rarely spoke to one another. During that time I never mentioned to anyone that I was married, legally or otherwise. It was my secret. Perhaps Sharon kept our marriage a secret too.

In my mind, I felt I had been faithful to Sharon. Outside of work, I was. But once our relationship fell apart there was no stopping me. I was on the ground floor of a booming industry, and I knew it. With work steadily coming my way, I performed in nameless 8mm loops, posed for magazine layouts, even doubled for actors in an occasional television series as a stuntman. The more I worked, the more people I met who introduced me to increasingly important people in the industry, such as producers, directors, moneymen. They all had one interest in common: pornography.

Sex was taking over my life. Films, however, were no longer my primary outlet. Over the next several years I became involved in numerous personal relationships. There was a girl from San Diego, a fiery redhead. Within a few weeks I was not only seeing her but her two redheaded sisters. Then I found myself with their redheaded mother. It worked out fine for awhile, at least until they started to talk and discovered I was doing all of them. Red heads - talk about tempers! It really didn't matter to me because there were other ladies waiting.

Husbands offered me money to fuck their wives, sometimes while they watched. Wives paid me to come back when their husbands weren't around. No matter where I went there was always someone new to meet, always some place to go, always a waiting bed.

New York was no different. I had thought my earlier stay there to visit my ex-Army buddy was living a fast life with nothing but girls, girls, girls. But that experience paled compared with what was to come. Since I had last seen Tony he had managed to work his way into a circle of "the right people." No pretending for Tony, only the real thing, the kind that drips money.

My entrée was immediate. I had no illusions as to why I was so readily accepted. I was still a nobody; I wasn't movie star gorgeous, and I had few social graces. These women were after one thing, and I knew it. Of course, what they wanted came at a price, but price was no obstacle and they were willing to pay handsomely.

The "circle" consisted mainly of divorcees and widows, patrons of the arts who seemed sympathetic when I'd tell them I was a starving actor trying to make my way into a Broadway production. The depth of their sympathy was of no consequence in their willingness to support me completely. At one point I was involved in simultaneous affairs with five dowagers. They were often less than satisfying but I was getting what I wanted, and I always gave my partners a good time. I had developed a technique as a teenager because of my size. It was during those years I discovered that because of my size, I had to go slower and spend more time on foreplay than other guys did. If I just jumped in the saddle I caused a woman pain, so I learned to take my time with extended foreplay to make her more receptive to me. My rule of thumb became: when a woman pulls me to her she was sufficiently lubricated to receive me.

I learned too that while a flat, muscular stomach may appeal to women visually, a slight bit of stomach is more exciting in bed. That's because even the slightest paunch adds friction and stimulation to the pubic area. Therefore, the more padding around a mans stomach, the more he will stimulate his partner. Beer, anyone?

Sexual gratification has never been that important to me, not while I was working, anyway. I was certainly working in New York, and the rewards were way beyond my expectations. I was on the receiving end of spectacular offerings: apartments furnished with priceless antiques, all leased in my name; Mercedes Benz automobiles; diamond-studded jewelry; and more cash than I could possibly spend. The biggest single haul came not from the daughter of a powerful crime figure but from a woman known to be as "rich as Rockefeller." I would have cleaned up even more had her attorneys not offered me fifty thousand dollars to "get lost." With the sisters from San Diego, I had begun to lead a double life. Now I was immersed in complications that were becoming impossible to keep secret. I took the money and returned to California. But the good times were far from over.

CHAPTER 5

Above the Sunset Strip in the Hollywood Hills, a new club had opened. Its name was Eden and it catered exclusively to couples and single women. Open only on weekends, Eden was an immediate sensation, often turning away as many as 2,000 customers a night. "You're a big reason for my success," the owner, a former cop, excitedly confided to me one evening. "You're the draw. People want to see you and meet you."

I didn't want to get caught up in the nightclub scene again when I was first asked to attend. I was filming, putting in long hours virtually each day of the week. But my weekends were free and I couldn't stay away. My inquisitive mind got the best of me, and I quickly became a regular.

The action at Eden was frantic. People somehow found their way there from all parts of the country to be a part of the "swinging singles" experience that was sweeping America. Eden was swinging, to be certain, everything from singular groping and nudity to group sex. I met some fascinating people, among them, a couple who offered me ten thousand dollars to father a child for them, a request I turned down.

Bored with the teeming activity, I began to stray from Eden to begin a series of relationships, fancying myself as "a romantic."

I was first smitten with an actress, then with a well-known pop singer. When those pairings failed I began seeing a really knockout lady with a sensational body. A dancer, she had starred in films and was currently headlining in Las Vegas. She was also unhappily married. For that reason we agreed never to have intimacies at her house, only at the apartment she had leased for me. Six months into our relationship, she invited me to her home. It was safe, she told me; her husband was away on business. Besides, we'd been drinking and everything was fine with the world.

My leggy friend and I were in bed when we heard a sound at the front door. Jumping from her arms stone naked, I grabbed my clothes and ran for the sliding glass door that led to the terrace. Outside in the darkness, as I began to step into my pants, I heard gunfire. Then I felt the searing pain in my leg. The force of the blow hurdled me over the terrace rail and down the ivy-covered hillside. Still naked but now blooded and in pain, I somehow managed to climb back up the slope to my car and drive to the nearest hospital, where I passed out on the steering wheel horn.

When I woke up I was facing two uniformed policemen who were full of questions about the gunshot wound. I was quiet for a long moment as I strained to come up with a possible alibi. Nothing made sense so I said with all the sincerity I could muster, "I'm a stunt man in the movies. I was rehearsing for a scene when my prop gun went off. I didn't know it was real."

The cops looked at each other, shaking their heads. I'm sunk, I told myself. Then one of the men said, "Stupid. Be careful next time."

"You're right," I answered. "And I will."

With that they were gone.

I let out a sigh of relief and began to relax. No more encounters with the police, I vowed silently. No more! I wanted to take my vow seriously, but somehow I couldn't. There was no way of predicting what the future held for me. I couldn't even predict what tomorrow would bring. Not so surprisingly, perhaps, my dancer friend continued to remain in my life. Or, rather, I continued to remain in hers when she divorced her husband and moved me into her house. Being a dancer, she knew all about legs. I couldn't have had a better therapist to get me back on my feet.

That relationship held yet another surprise for me, however. After nearly a year together she let one of her dainty shoes drop. She had secretly remarried and was supporting her new husband in Las Vegas. How was I to know she was seeing another man during her frequent trips away for headlining performances? It was time for me to move on.

More despondent than I cared to admit over the breakup, I became a regular at the bars of Beverly Hills' posh hotels where I became chummy with the bartenders. "You get a lot of lonely, rich old ladies looking for some action," I told them. "*I'm* the action. Fix me up and I'll cut you in on the take." I met some fascinating ladies and received the usual expensive gifts, including complimentary "vacations" for two to such destinations as London, Paris and Rome, but I was like dead meat on a rack. I had lost all enthusiasm for what I was doing. I was smoking and drinking more than ever.

I had come to what I believed was a turning point. "Do I want to work in films," I asked myself, "or be a whore?" My private life was going nowhere while my work in adult films seemed to be heading in new directions.

The sexual revolution was reaching an all-time high. Within the Los Angeles area, a number of individuals were beginning to organize companies and invest huge amounts of money in the making of adult entertainment. Theaters were opening in major cities for the exclusive showing of porno movies. Following the release of such films as Deep Throat and The Devil in Miss Jones, branded obscene but upheld by the courts, the public no longer seemed to have a problem with being seen in lines at porno movie houses. Unlike the days of seedy-looking men with long trench coats, it had actually become acceptable for couples, even groups of friends, to attend such places. Porn had suddenly become a part of popular culture.

Between all my running around and whoring, I had made a handful of feature films myself. The names of the earliest ones are long forgotten, but I believe The Ladies Bed Companion was among the first.

Feature movies were definitely a step above loop life. Scripts weren't necessary to churn out a loop; besides, scripts were evidence if found in a raid. Now we were given actual pages with story lines and dialogue to memorize. And we had shooting schedules, days instead of hours.

I had met Hawaiian-born director Bob Chinn in 1970. Now, several years later, I ran into him again. "I'm making another porn flick," Chinn told me, "and I'd love for you to be in it." What Bob had in mind, I didn't know. But he certainly came along at the right time.

The chance encounter led to my being cast as Johnny Wadd, a no-nonsense, gun-toting private eye a la Dirty Harry, whose capers led him into more beds than dark alleys. At first, Chinn had no name for his character. We were standing around MacArthur Park in Los Angeles one afternoon when he asked me if I had any ideas what to call the film. "Why not name the lead guy Johnny Wadd," I suggested. "And that could be the title of the film."

Being of Chinese descent, Bob didn't immediately understand what "Johnny Wadd" implied. But after trying it out on a few people he got the message and decided to use it.

Johnny Wadd was my first real screen characterization and Johnny Wadd, Detective, my first film with Bob Chinn, was a great working experience for me. It had a plot with substance, a large cast and crew, a six-week shooting schedule, a big budget, and location filming. For the first time I had a chance to work away from sheltered studio walls.

Bob and I made a good team. He allowed me to shape my character, whose trademarks were a big dick and a pinkie ring (an enormous diamond encrusted dragonfly that had been given to me as a reward from a lady friend for "services rendered"), in addition to giving me free reign in the creation of my sex scenes. I didn't tell Bob how to edit and he didn't tell me how to fuck.

Following Johnny Wadd, Detective, we made Ensenada

Wadd on location in Mexico. Filming on location has its drawbacks, as we soon discovered. While in Ensenada to shoot prison conditions and squalid street scenes for background shots, we were threatened with arrest for working without a permit. Facing a possible five-year jail sentence, we were able to escape only because our newer revved up engines could outrun the posse.

While in Hawaii for Waikiki Wadd, I signed a contract to work nights at a dingy downtown Honolulu club performing simulated sex on stage with an attractive young partner. We never did anything but we were nude and the act was choreographed to such a point that it was highly erotic. The girl and I created such a sensation that the club owner kept renewing our options.

The act continued long after the completion of Waikiki Wadd. In fact, months passed and I had to return to Hollywood for the start of another film. I gave the club owner two weeks notice, but he would not let me go. The next thing I knew I was being arrested on lewd conduct charges and headed for a trial, which lasted five months. It seemed odd to me that while I was free on bail I was allowed to continue performing at the club. It seemed less odd when I realized that I had been set up by the club owner. With one phone call to a friend at the police department, he got what he wanted: more of me and a lot of free publicity.

Johnny Wadd pushed me into the limelight. I had more offers to appear in films than I could handle, and that wasn't all. I was wanted for personal appearances at various Miss Nude USA contests, film premiers, trade shows, as well as for numerous endorsements and magazine interviews. Whenever I showed up at a public event the atmosphere was like a carnival. People were lined up around the block to get my autograph. Men asked me to autograph their wives' breasts. I had women asking me to deflower their daughters. "How big is it?" fans would scream.

"Bigger than a pay phone, smaller than a Cadillac," was my stock reply.

I was traveling all over the world with all expenses paid and making thousands of dollars just to sign my name and promote movies. The women in other parts of the world were just as hot, if not hotter, than the women in America.

I had become the biggest name in adult films; the highest paid performer in the industry. The John Wayne of pornography. And I was working my ass off, often in risky situations. One producer got me stranded in the dead of night on a remote California desert. There I was, fighting off millions of ants and bees, without any clothes on. Then there was the time a knife-wielding leading lady took the director literally when he yelled, "Cut!" I've been filmed having sex atop rocky ledges, rooftops, pianos, the hoods of cars and a Paris Metro platform, aboard airplanes, boats, trains, helicopters and, of all places, at the corner of Hollywood and Vine. I love to work in bed, but I've gone through phases where they've put me in the most insane settings. That makes it more exciting, for everyone, I suppose, except for the person who has to make it happen.

CHAPTER 6

It was cash, always cash, even as my asking price began escalating out of sight. As a result, I had more cash than any human had a right to possess. Not being a spendthrift, it was important for me to invest the money wisely. I began by putting together a stock portfolio, then adding apartment buildings one by one. I also opened a combination antique shop and locksmith service, to be run by my half-brother, David. We stocked it with many of the riches I had accumulated in my trick pads along with some interesting pieces from my junk collections.

Some years earlier, David had started to visit me during his annual summer school breaks. By the third summer, David was begging to stay. He was only fifteen, but he didn't want to return to Ohio to face Harold. Still unable to forget the brutal treatment I had received from his hands, I agreed to let David stay, but only with the approval of our mother.

Mom was terrific, just as sympathetic as she had been when I had decided to bolt at an early age. She even offered to arrange the transfer of David's school transcripts. From then on David had been my responsibility. I saw him through high school and financed his further education at a trade school. Now I was setting him up in business.

I even had a hand in David's sex education. Shortly after his sixteenth birthday he came to me wanting to talk. "I've never been laid," he confessed, with a hangdog look.

Who better to solve his problem than Johnny Wadd?

A phone call was all it took to set him up with a younger lady whom I could personally vouch for as being quite lusty in bed. Never having observed any of my brothers at full mast, I was naturally inquisitive to catch the pair in action. Seeing David, it became obvious real fast that we had more in common than the same mother.

David taught me a lesson, as well. For two years he had been pushing me to try marijuana. Because of a childhood illness, he had occasionally smoked a joint. I didn't try to stop him because I knew he had a fairly good reason to use the stuff when necessary, but it wasn't for me. I'd had chances before, many times. Ever since I got into adult films hardly a day passed that I didn't have offers to do drugs. All I had to do was walk on a set. But David kept pushing, and what do you know? I liked it.

The issue came up again on my next shoot when I was hired for two films to be shot on location in France. One was a remake of <u>Beauty and the Beast</u> and the other, <u>The New Henry Miller,</u> in which I was to play the American writer delving into the vices of French aristocracy. We had a seventeen-week schedule with a combined budget of just under one million dollars. That included my fee of fifteen hundred dollars each day I worked and nine hundred dollars per day off, plus all expenses.

Drugs, especially the lack of marijuana, became a hot topic of conversation among the Americans. None of the cast or crew had dared to bring anything with them fearing a search at the airport and possible imprisonment in a foreign country. Who knew that when you flew into DeGaulle Airport they had only one guy waving everybody through? I could have brought an atomic bomb into France and no one would have noticed.

We had all the wine we could drink, but that didn't come close to satisfying everyone's craving for "weed." In desperation, we contacted an actress involved in the filming who was scheduled for a later arrival in France. "Pack a pound in a suitcase," we told her. "It's perfectly safe." She agreed, but on arrival she was empty-handed, having backed out at the last minute.

It was left to a black dwarf from Haiti, who was part of a Fellini-like orgy scene, to finally arrange a sale of African marijuana. After all that trouble, it turned out to be very expensive and no stronger than catnip.

The long overseas shoot was tiring, buoyed only by wine and the inferior narcotic. Many nights were spent alone in my chateau bedroom putting down thoughts and ideas that raced through my head, trying my hand at poetry and short stories. I went crazy in France. It was if a writer from hundreds of years ago had possessed me.

A heavy filming schedule was facing me back in the United States. Still, I was glad to see New York City, where I lingered for personal appearances and to visit a few friends. It was impossible to hit New York without seeing my old Army buddy, Tony, while I was there, but finding him wasn't easy. I finally tracked him down at a hole-in-the-wall diner in an ugly neighborhood. He was working behind the counter. For a second I felt like I was back washing dishes at the hot dog stand on Hollywood Boulevard.

I don't know what kind of greeting I expected, but a simple "hello" or a "glad to see you again" would have been nice. Instead, Tony's first words were to ask me for a loan. That didn't surprise me as much as his appearance. Once handsome and trim, Tony was now bloated, skin-topped and foul smelling. His hair, what he had left, looked greasier than the slop he was dishing out.

Before I had a chance to ask, Tony was telling me about his streak of bad luck: two failed marriages and two years in jail for forgery to feed his drug habit. The reunion was depressing, as were the phone calls I received pleading for money long after I returned to California.

Back at work, it was one feature film after another in rapid succession for me, partnered with such leading ladies as Marilyn Chambers, Candy Samples, Renee Bond, Uschi Dagard, Serena and Seka. Feature length films gave audiences the chance to choose their favorite stars, and once a star was in demand, his or her price went up, up, up. I was lucky to be paired with the most beautiful and talented women appearing in adult films. Of course, it takes more than beauty and talent. Believability is a major factor. Some women can make a part so believable you don't know they are acting. But if a girl is there just to make money to pay the rent, or she hates being under hot lights, or she doesn't even like guys, it shows. Renee Bond was absolutely the best, however, because she *loved* to give head. She sucked cock like a starving orphan with her first candy-cane. You were a gob of goo when she got through with you.

I was also lucky to be a male star. Men seem to thrive in the business for ten years or more, while women seem to last only several years, at best. Women get frustrated with the hours and the travel, and with having men constantly in their faces. Or they run into guys who are worth millions and disappear. The hours and the travel can indeed wear you down, especially when you're jumping from one film to another, hundreds within a single year. That didn't bother me the first few years. I liked being in demand, I craved it. I had something to sell, and sell I did.

One day, however, I confided to a producer, "I'm so tired I can hardly move." His name was Bill. Being in the business we saw each other frequently, and it wasn't long before we became fast friends. He even named me as God-Father to his children. I began spending a lot of time at Bill's big house on the hill; it was the perfect party pad. With Bill, the producer, and me, Mr. Porno Stud, girls were drawn to us like bees to honey. His wild nudist romps, especially in the heat of summer around his pool, were the raging ticket in town. The girls didn't mind who they fucked, just as long as we wanted them or they thought it would get them in movies. There was only one problem: sex, sex and more sex!

I had done nothing but have sex for years, and I was getting tired. Tired of never getting any sleep, that is. But more than sleep I needed an energy boost.

Bill smiled at my confession and disappeared for a minute. When he returned, he held out his hand. "Here, take this," he said. It was a small rock of cocaine. "Try it and you'll be back on your feet."

In the past I had always responded to such offers with a firm "I don't do drugs." Sure, I had smoked pot over the years but that was as far as I went. This time, however, I didn't say no.

The first taste was awful, a real put-off. But then a wonderful thing happened, and that was the catcher. I found that I was able to stay awake longer, and think better, and be more stimulated sexually. "This is just what I need," I told myself. "It's not hurting me, it's helping me."

That was my early reaction. But within three months I discovered that I had to increase my intake in order to achieve the same high performance level. The three hundred dollars a week I was spending on coke increased to five hundred, then one thousand.

Like my craving for sex had spun wildly out of control over a ten-year period, so had my newly found habit. Looking back, it would be so easy to place the blame on Bill for offering me that initial "pick me up." But unlike Linda Lovelace, I can honestly say that no one held a gun to my head. No one in the business ever forced me to do anything I didn't want to do.

Once I had agreed to try drugs, they were everywhere I went, on the set and off. And, just like sex, no matter where I turned, someone was offering me a silver spoonful. At the height of my addiction, I was free-basing at a cost of $1,500 a day. It took a few years, but I was on my way to losing everything to finance my addiction. First I sold the stocks and bonds, then the apartment buildings, then the stores. And because my attitude had changed, I even lost friends and associates.

For over fifteen years I had prided myself on being the most reliable performer in the adult film industry. Now I began showing up late on sets, looking glassy-eyed and gaunt, having dropped thirty pounds. Slim to begin with, I had turned into a rail.

It was during this period that I filmed <u>Exhausted.</u> The story line should have been a romp for me, as it was supposedly *my* story, a real semidocumentary based on my life. During the on-camera interviews I could barely remember who I was or where I was, so I made up lies. Lies about where I was born, my family, everything. I couldn't remember the simplest lines, or wait for the filming to end. In the middle of a scene I would disappear for long stretches, but my co-workers knew where to find me: in the bathroom doing freebase. I became the butt of jokes, which traveled around like wildfire. "To get Holmes to work," they said, "you have to leave a trail of freebase from the bathroom to the bedroom."

Things got worse for me. With money growing increasingly short, I began looking for things to steal. It started somewhat low-key by going through an old girlfriend's purse. Soon I found myself rummaging through, even breaking into cars. I was always looking for things to steal. I couldn't remember lines, but I knew the location of every hockshop in town.

John "Cash" Holmes had become John "Crash" Holmes.

CHAPTER 7

The brown-haired girl stood near a freeway off-ramp in Hollywood with her thumb hanging out. It was a warm spring afternoon and she was showing a lot of skin.

I'll give anybody a ride as long as the person is female and fairly attractive. This one was both. She was also young, still in her teens, and wearing a clinging, off-white tank top that left little to the imagination, falling loosely over her bare shoulders. I couldn't stop the van fast enough. "Where are you heading?" I shouted through the open window.

She moved closer and peeked inside. Her eyes had a strange look about them. She may have been young enough to be a schoolgirl but no question, she'd been up and down the freeway, and a few other fast roads, more than once. Without saying a word, she opened the passenger door and hopped in beside me. "I know who you are," she said, checking me over.

"Yeah?"

"Yeah, you're the guy with the big dick. You're in dirty pictures."

"Have you ever seen any?"

"Sure," she answered smugly, as if they were required viewing. Then she curled up in her seat, facing me, and stared long and hard. "Are you really that guy...John Holmes?"

"Want me to prove it?" Half jokingly, I reached for my fly.

"Do you do any coke?"

Do I do coke? Hey, kid how would you like a quick rundown of all the money I've blown on the stuff? You think I look this way from wheat germ and alfalfa sprouts? I should have been as outspoken with her as she was being with me. Instead, I kept my mouth shut and nodded responsively - a conditioned reflex, no doubt - as my eyes scanned her enticing young body. Her nipples appeared to be small and firm as they poked against the flimsy material.

"So do I," she said intently, "but I'm out."

Under the dash, in a dark crevice, I kept a small plastic pouch. I withdrew it, and for the next several minutes we sat parked along the curb, oblivious to the passing traffic, exchanging "hits."

Had I known what I was getting myself into I would have said a quick good-bye and driven away. Alone. But I didn't, and when she wanted to know "Which way are you heading from here?" I got cute. "I asked you first, remember?"

Her blank expression told me she didn't.

"Forget it," I said, getting serious, "I'm heading west. I was on my way to pick up some coke when you came along."

"How far west?

"It doesn't matter. Where do you want to go?" I fingered the ignition key, then turned it. The motor began to purr.

"Some friends of mine have the best coke in the world."

"No, darlin'." I countered, "a friend of <u>mine</u> has the best coke in the world. But who's arguing, right? Just tell me where and we're on our way. I've got nothing but time."

She pointed down Sunset Boulevard and we were off, blending into the slow-moving procession of cars. At Laurel Canyon, opposite Schwab's Drug Store, she motioned for me to turn right. The traffic lessened now as the road became more treacherous, a succession of hairpin curves that snaked upward into the hills. We passed residential side streets with Pollyanna names like Honey Drive, Lark Lane and Merrywood Terrace, climbing through wooded areas and open stretches of tinder-dry brush. I hadn't a clue to where she was leading me, but I soon found out.

Reaching Lookout Mountain, a remote, narrow road several miles short of the summit, I was instructed to turn left. Moments later we were veering off onto Wonderland Avenue. My young companion straightened in her seat. "We're here," she said. "Stop."

The developers of the area obviously had a dream that backfired. Wonderland it wasn't. Not even Bel Air or Beverly Hills. There were no sprawling mansions of imported stone, marble or brick. I saw no vast grounds or landscapes punctuated by fountains, pools or lush plantings, no sweeping terrazzo driveways, and no courtyards. Not even one <u>porte-cochere.</u> Here the homes were made of stucco and wood, crowded into the hillsides, neglected, in need of paint or general repair. More often than not, the landscaping was Nature's own; overgrown, running wild. The sounds echoing across the hills came not from catering trucks and gardener's mowers but from the barking of neighborhood dogs on the loose.

Slowly, I maneuvered the van up an incline before a bilious green two-story house. With a paint job like that it didn't really need any further identification. It had some anyway: four numbers - 8763 - marked with uncertain strokes on the door frame. "I'll be right back," the young girl said, bounding from my side. "I want to tell everyone we're here."

"What do you mean _we're_ here?" I called after her. "I'm just dropping you off." I had no intention of following her inside.

She stopped in the center of the roadway, the bright overhead sun playing against the soft curves of her body, and turned sharply. "Oh, please, she begged, "you've got to come in." For the first time since we met, she sounded like a real kid.

The place looked deserted. "How do you know anyone's home?"

"They're always home," she said knowingly. "They're always shooting up."

She painted a beautiful picture. Maybe this was wonderland after all.

In less time than it took me to turn off the ignition and roll up the windows, she was back, opening the driver's door and tugging at my arm with youthful exuberance. "Come on, <u>come on</u>," she prodded, excitedly, "they're dying to meet you." This time she didn't get any feedback.

Inside, the house was a foul-smelling shambles. It was difficult to see much with the shades drawn, but neglect was evident everywhere. Sections of newspapers - too many for a single day's delivery - were scattered across the floor and furniture. Half-filled glasses and dishes smeared with decaying remnants of meals past nestled on table tops along with crumpled bags of potato chips, cigarette packs and ashtrays filled to overflowing. In the empty spaces, overturned shoes, socks and other odd pieces of discarded clothing appeared to substitute for bedding for the two raging Staffordshire terriers - pit bulls - at our feet.

"They're all bark," came a voice from above, "just kick 'em off if they give you trouble." A light was on upstairs where three people stood gawking over a spindly balustrade. One of them waved us up and we made the climb. For the next few minutes I was grabbed, fondled, squeezed, hugged, petted and patted. I heard my name mentioned no less than a half-dozen times. The recognition, and attention, pleased me.

The one doing most of the feeling was a woman named Joy Miller. Like the house itself, she was desperately in need of a good once-over. She wore no makeup and her hennaed hair was stringy and limp, no telling when it had last been exposed to a comb, let alone soap or water. Her eyes were puffy and darkly lined, as was the rest of her face. Even when she smiled, which wasn't all that often, she appeared tired and haggard. Old beyond her years.

Joy, I soon discovered, shared the Wonderland house with two men, Billy Deverell and Ronny Launius. No one shared Joy; she was Billy's exclusive property. Billy and Joy were similar in several ways. Both were short and in their mid-to late forties. It's possible that Joy colored her hair to look closer in age to Billy. On the other hand, Billy's jet-black hair was streaked with gray, which tended to make him more a match for his "old lady."

Although Ronny, the baby of the trio, was seven or eight years younger than his roommates, the gap seemed narrower. His thinning blond hair didn't help. Neither did his cold, steely eyes and spacey expression. A tall man, six feet or more, Ronny towered over Billy. They made an odd combination: the Mutt and Jeff of the drug world.

Joy, Billy and Ronny each had a long history of arrests, a fact I didn't discover until later. That probably wouldn't have bothered me, had I known from the start. My slate wasn't all that clean either.

These people were scum, the poorest excuses imaginable for humanity, in my opinion - now, of course. Had I met them a year or two earlier I would have turned and run. But times had changed. I'd changed. To my distorted way of thinking, they represented security and camaraderie. I was short on friends. When they reached out I wanted to grab hold.

Getting close to the Wonderland three-some wasn't at all difficult. In fact, I became part of "the family" that very afternoon. It happened the minute I forked over $500 for a quarter-ounce of cocaine.

Over the next few months, 8763 became my hangout, my hideout, my crash pad. My apartment was gone; without a job, no money or offers coming in, I'd had to give it up. For the first time in over ten years, producers were snubbing me. I was poison, unpredictable, and irresponsible. It didn't help that I looked like death warmed over. I couldn't even sustain an erection. Nobody wanted a hophead - or a limp phallic symbol.

Money became so tight that I was forced to sell my van. With part of the money, I bought David's beat-up Chevy

Malibu. David accepted the cash on the spot, just as he'd accepted the car as a gift fresh from the showroom.

My new best friends saw to it that my pockets were never empty. I became their star delivery boy - a drug runner making clandestine calls to some of Hollywood's most famous addresses. Showing up at a bigwig's house with a pound of cocaine and one hundred base pipes for his celebrity guests wasn't unusual. Not all of my clients were in show business. It didn't matter what they did or who they were as long as they had the bucks.

Buying a stash from John Holmes (or "Betty Crocker," my code name) became a real kick. See Mr. Big. See the Porn King. Fast-fading royalty, live - functioning, anyway - and in person. He really delivers!

For my efforts, I was paid in nugget-sized rocks of base worth a thousand dollars. The trouble was, I had to "earn" that much every day just to sustain my own habit - not that I was irrevocably hooked. I never believed <u>that</u> for an instant. Nor was I overly concerned about my expenses. By comparison, the two grand that Joy, Billy and Ronny each shot away daily made me look small time. We weren't even close to being in the same league.

While making my rounds I became exposed to an underground that I never dreamed existed. Most of the people I dealt with on a drug level lived in quiet, residential neighborhoods. From the outside, their homes or apartments looked perfectly respectable. On the inside, however, they were armed camps containing entire rooms filled with crates of automatic weapons, shrapnel grenades and ammunition, suitcases packed with counterfeit money, boxes and bags crammed with jewelry and narcotics.

These people made their money by stealing, primarily Mercedes Benz cars, which they repainted and outfitted with new serial numbers, then shipped to other states and countries. (Hawaii was a favorite destination.) The cash they received was turned over to me for drugs that they wanted or needed to buy something else.

There's a subculture of trading in America that the general public knows little or nothing about. Each of the states, and many cities within them have separate bands of burglars, armed robbers, car thieves, arms dealers, and counterfeit money traders. These groups have several common links: they're all terrified of the police, they're all resentful of authority, and they all deal in narcotics and money.

Narcotics and money are their stock in trade, and they need both to operate. For instance, if you want to buy a submachine gun, you can pay cash or trade drugs for it. To get the drugs you need money. To make money you need drugs. The two go hand in fist.

An endless supply of counterfeit money was available. At one point, I heard that $3 million in bogus bills was being pumped into the County of Los Angeles over a two-day period. The connection was offering to trade real dollars for counterfeit at a five-to-one ratio, and word had it that takers from as far away as New York and Chicago were lining up at his back door to make the switch. ($10,000 in real money brought them $50,000 in hard-to-detect fake $100 and $50 bills.) From the connection's house, the fake paper made its way into the stores in exchange for such inexpensive items as chewing gum or cigarettes. The pressure was always on to make the exchange as rapidly as possible, then back off before the Feds had time to find out where the dealings were taking place. Otherwise, they'd swarm in hot and heavy.

Because guns were so highly prized and in demand, they were often preferred as barter. Uzi and Thompson submachine guns could bring up to three times the going rate in counterfeit money.

God have mercy on anyone who created problems for the connections. Virtually every group had an enforcer to clamp down on troublemakers. The most common "victims" were customers who were unable to pay their huge and mounting drug debts.

Enforcers were known for their unique, persuasive methods of collecting money. One had a notorious reputation for using hot irons. If the customer wasn't home, he would grab anyone who answered the door - usually the customer's wife - strip her and tie her down on the floor, then place a steam iron on her stomach. He'd plug it in and walk out the door, leaving the iron to cook its way through her guts.

Driving from place to place I'd often see stores with massive "Going Out of Business" signs plastered across the windows. The next time I'd pass by, the building would be a charred rubble, burned to the ground. The stores had been torched for the insurance money, with the owner's full cooperation. There was talk on the streets that one powerful dealer had "his man" torch two and three shops and office buildings a week.

In time, the Wonderland people had their own enforcer, a bullnecked, powerfully built and heavily-tattooed wrestler type who'd spent more time in jail than out. I called him Karl but he answered to "the bounty hunter," a label he'd proudly pinned on himself. Karl had two great passions in life, killing anyone who got in his way, and torturing women. To look at him, with his chilling, stone gray eyes, was like standing naked on a block of ice in a meat freezer. If Karl came to the door selling encyclopedias, dressed in his Sunday clothes, you'd call the police.

Several months after I'd been invited into the Wonderland house, Ronny Launius and Billy Deverall began flying to Sacramento "on business." Actually, they'd gotten into some kind of trouble and had to appear in court. They were ultimately absolved, but they didn't catch the first plane home; they lingered long enough to try and set up a big narcotics deal, dropping a bundle of money in the process. Infuriated, they took to a local bar to plot their revenge.

It was in the Sacramento bar that they met "the bounty hunter." Karl had overheard their heated conversation, introduced himself, and offered to get their money back. Ronny and Billy were so impressed with Karl's awesome presence and intimidating tactics that they invited him to

Hollywood to strong-arm their debtors there. Karl accepted on the spot and Wonderland had a frightening new family member.

When I wasn't making my rounds, I'd flop around the Wonderland house, half-stoned in faded jeans and a crumpled shirt, either watching television with Joy, a slovenly portrait herself in slippers and a tattered, shapeless housecoat (she'd lost both breasts to cancer) or hovering around Ronny while he sharpened his knives. Ronny had one of the biggest collections in Hollywood even before he'd had a walk-on in a Sylvester Stallone movie and ripped off half the props. His prize was a custom-made combat knife worth $350.00.

Watching TV was impossible if Billy and Ronny happened to be in the room. They never stopped talking. If they weren't planning drug deals or discussing persuasive methods of collecting bad debts with Karl, they were boasting about their latest heist. Hardly a day passed that they didn't knock over a gas station, corner market, liquor store, pawnshop or residence to bring in extra cash. For kicks, they'd often wind up a successful outing by snatching a purse from some helpless victim on the street.

Life at Wonderland was seldom dull. The doorbell rang at all hours, day and night, pushed by shifty-eyed strangers after a quick fix or a take-out. Joy deftly doled out the drugs and raked in the profits.

The majority of visitors stayed only briefly. Others, many of them regulars, lingered on to join in the evening drug feast, wild and frantic, stereo-blasting affairs that had the revelers (and nearby neighbors, no doubt) climbing the walls.

During the months that I spent at 8763, so many people passed in and out the front door - hundreds upon hundreds - that faces became featureless blurs. Names, when offered, which was seldom, were soon forgotten. There were two notable exceptions.

Susan Launius also came from Sacramento. Her reason for visiting the house was far different than Barbara's, however. She came to try and patch things up with Ronny, her estranged husband. They'd talk behind closed doors or go off together briefly to get away from the rat race. Then they'd reappear, unsmiling and silent once more. They never seemed to make any headway. Ronny had more pressing matters on his mind. We all did. Like "basing," and partying, and growing old.

"What's that?" Joy growled, staring through half-open lids at the plastic bag that Billy carried through the front door. Sprawled limply across the living room sofa, she looked awful, worse than usual. She needed a fix bad. So did the others. "This will get us feeling good again, babe," Billy said. "We scored big this time."

Joy struggled to prop herself up on an elbow. "Yeah? What have you got there?"

Billy set the bag on the floor beside her and pulled out a handful of glittering gold chains and three heavy handguns.

"Jesus," she groaned, "haven't we got enough of that shit already?"

"Nothing like this," Ronny said. "The chains are solid gold and the guns are antiques. They're worth **real** money."

The guns did look old, but there was no way of telling if they were as valuable as Ronny made them sound. He called them "museum pieces" and said that they once belonged to "some historical figure." He kept mentioning Davy Crockett's name, although he had no proof.

"Well, do something with them," Joy snapped, "and hurry up about it."

Billy's face twisted with rage. He tolerated Joy's testiness during withdrawal only because he could so easily identify with what she was going through. Still, he often acted as if he wanted to slug her. He never did, as far as I know - not that she would have felt anything, being so out of it. He usually turned away, as he did this time to toss the stolen merchandise back in the bag. Then he pointed to me and said, "Take this stuff over to your Arab friend and see what you can do."

I was dealing mostly in cocaine and marijuana, but "my Arab friend," Nash, had a tight heroin connection. Like the Wonderland people, Nash was hooked on heroin. He was also heavily into speedballing, though not by injection. He'd freebase heroin and cocaine, mix them up and smoke the substance in a bubble pipe. (It was speedballing that killed John Belushi nine months later.)

Eddie Nash was one of my connections. I had met him several years earlier at the Seven Seas, a club he owned on Hollywood Boulevard across from Mann's Chinese Theatre. Eddie was into pornography in a big way; he also happened to be a big fan of mine. It made him happy to introduce me to his customers and it made me happy to set him up with women. In exchange he supplied me with coke.

It took approximately five minutes to get to Nash's latest residence - he moved every other month, it seemed, for security reasons - a sprawling, spacious, very private one-story ranch house. He too now lived off Laurel Canyon, although on the other side of the hill, overlooking the San Fernando Valley.

Before leaving Wonderland, I called to make sure that I'd be welcome. Nash did not like visitors dropping in unexpectedly. Neither did the burly bodyguards who roamed about his place at all hours.

The guns and jewelry brought an immediate expression of interest from Nash, along with a wariness to accept the merchandise. For several long moments, he paced nervously from one end of his enormous living room to the other, at times seemingly lost as his diminutive frame moved between huge, overstuffed pieces of furniture. When at last he came to a stop, he turned abruptly and said, "No, I don't want what you've brought me. How am I going to handle it?"

More jewelry had passed through Nash's hands than over

the counters of Cartier. I'd seen coat hangers strung with hundreds of stolen wedding rings, and bags of precious stones - diamonds, rubies, emeralds, and sapphires - marked to be sold. The gold mountings that had held the priceless gems had been melted into bricks and sent to Iran in exchange for shipments of guns. I knew more about Nash's operation than I wanted to share with him. "You're the one with the connections," I told him.

"The guns are worth real money, sure, seventy-five grand maybe, but they're too easy to spot. I could never unload them." He started pacing again, working his way toward the huge picture window with its spectacular view of the valley below. He stood there for several moments, motionless and silent, with his back to me. "I don't like this," he said, sharply, "but here's what I'll do." His eyes narrowed as he moved closer. "I'll hold the guns and jewelry for seven days in exchange for an advance of one thousand dollars. You can take the money and get the heroin from somebody else to hold your friends over."

"A thousand dollars?" I said, stunned. He was offering nothing - or, at least next to nothing. The Wonderland people could shoot up a grand of heroin in a few hours. "The merchandise is worth much more than that," I argued. "You said so yourself."

Nash's expression hardened. "Let me tell you something, Mr. Movie Star. I don't like dealing with heroin people. They're not like cocaine people. When cocaine people run out of cocaine - and cash - they won't try to kill somebody for the money they need to supply their habit. Heroin people are different. They'll knock off a cop to get his badge if they think it's worth anything. I know you understand." He grabbed one of the antique guns and began fingering it.

"I understand," I replied quietly.

"Good," he said, nodding. "Then I'll advance you the money for your friends on Wonderland - but only for seven days. And if they start giving you a bad time, or causing you trouble, come to me. **You tell me** - is that clear? I'll handle it."

Nash was a great salesman. I'd come away with a paltry sum, not what I'd expected, but he made me feel as if I'd just negotiated a major coup. I had his complete backing, or so he said, and I wouldn't be returning to Wonderland empty-handed. It sounded like a no risk situation. How could I lose?

Seven days passed, then fourteen. Nash's financed supply of heroin at Wonderland was long gone. Everyone was growing progressively more desperate, getting sick on withdrawal, even though they were seldom without drugs for long stretches. Billy, Ronny and Karl saw to that. Over the two-week period they must have ripped off twenty-five people. They'd run shouting through the house while tracking down their guns, and then tear off half-crazed to cruise the streets in search of money to feed their habits. On their return, the men would take a position on the second-floor balcony, their guns poised and their eyes riveted to the street searching for cops. A few minutes of that was long enough to satisfy them that they hadn't been followed. Getting back inside, and slamming heroin, took priority over everything.

They were in a constant frenzy, at times so filled with tension that I half expected their spines to shatter from the strain. It wasn't all due to drugs, or the thought of being caught.

None of the stolen money was earmarked for Nash. Part of it went for heroin; the rest went to pay off another powerful drug source, who can not be named here. I'll call him Sam.

The Wonderland people were into Sam for $125,000, and Sam wanted his money back. Hardly a day went by that Sam wasn't on the phone to Billy or Ronny demanding that he be paid in full. There were loud, screaming arguments followed by quick, desperate departures into the streets for money. One call ended with Sam demanding that they come up with the cash within a week. If they failed to deliver, he threatened to knock over the Wonderland house. Sam always made good on his threats.

As the due date drew nearer, Billy and Ronny, especially, became more frantic than ever. Raising the enormous sum of cash that they needed through their daily heists was impossible, which left them not only clawing at the walls, but at each other. There was only one way that they could make Sam's deadline, they figured, and that was by getting their guns and jewelry back from Nash and fencing the goods for an astronomical amount. They became obsessed with the thought.

"There's only one hitch," I told them. "Nash won't part with anything until you repay the thousand dollars he loaned you."

Billy and Ronny weren't the least bit concerned about the money. They wanted only to get their hands on the merchandise.

I listened but said nothing to Nash, not until the Wonderland men started making threats of their own. "Tell your connection that we want our stuff back or there's going to be trouble," they said. "Let him know we'll pay up *after* the sale is made." They were feeding me a line of crap, but I wasn't about to argue with them, not with "killer Karl" breathing down my neck. Nash would never see his money. Sam would get it. Or they'd shoot it on drugs.

Nash took the message from Wonderland in stride. "Those assholes don't scare me," he said with a smirk. "They don't even know how to find me - and you're not going to tell them, are you?"

"No."

"Good - then stay calm and stop worrying."

That night, Billy, Ronny and Karl devised a plan to get their merchandise back - by ripping off Nash's house - and I was to help them gain entry. The idea was for me to get

Nash to open his front door while they hid in the bushes. Once the door was open, they'd rush him and storm inside.

The plan was CRAZY - and full of holes. For one thing, Nash rarely opened his own door. For another, no one answered the door without a gun in his hand. Even if they were able to get inside, they'd run head-on into Nash's bodyguards, including his main man, 300-pounds of black sludge named Gregory Diles.

"It won't work," I said, emphatically. "There will be a bloody shoot-out. You'll never get out alive."

"We'll make it!" Karl growled, flexing his muscles.

"Don't count on it," I said, sharply. "The guy lives on a cul-de-sac. The police will be there in thirty seconds. Even if you do get out, you'll be trapped. The only way to make it work is to sneak in, and catch *everybody* by surprise."

"Then figure out a way," Billy said, anxiously. "Just get us into that goddamn house!"

"Yeah, **you** get us in," Karl snapped, "or we'll blow your fucking head off!" He sounded desperate enough to do just that.

"Okay, calm down," I replied. "I'll see what I can work out."

I had no intention of doing anything. I'd already done enough to help them. Too much.

Thank God Nash was on my side. "The Wonderland people are getting way out of hand," I told him. "They want to come here and hold you up. They are serious. They're packing heavy, and pissed off!"

The little Arab was on a freebase jag and hadn't slept in ten days. "That's **your** problem," he hissed, half out if his mind.

"They're coming to get their goods," I shot back, "and they'll do anything to get them."

Nash's face reddened. "Get the hell out of my life! The

guns are <u>mine</u> now. The jewelry's <u>mine</u>. Fuck off!" He started to lunge for me but I backed away, then made for the door. It was no use arguing with him in his present state.

I couldn't let the matter drop. Somehow, I had to make Nash listen to me. There had to be a way out to avoid the bloodbath that was set to take place.

I returned to Nash's house twice more that day in the late afternoon to warn him once again (if anything he was even less receptive), then in the evening to try a different approach. "If the Wonderland people can't pay you," I said, "I'll raise the money. Let me pay off their debt."

"Sure....fine," Nash snickered, "but you waited too long."

"What do you mean?"

"The agreement was for one week. Now the price has doubled."

"How am I going to come up with that much cash, for Christ's sake?"

"Wait another week and the price will be three thousand."

"Damn it, we're running out of time! Give me the guns <u>now</u> and there won't be any trouble. I'll see that you get paid."

Nash started to curl up on the couch, then changed his mind. Calling to one of his bodyguards, he announced, "Close up and lock everybody out. I'm going to bed." Turning on his shiny, black elevated heels, he disappeared in the direction of his bedroom.

The little bastard! Over the past year I'd given him over a half a million dollars. He'd taken everything I'd ever owned. He owed me, and yet he wouldn't trust me for a lousy grand or two.

"Waiting for something?" a voice asked from behind me. It belonged to Nash's top gun, Diles.

"I have to hit the head," I told him, "then I'm out of here." He shrugged and stood his ground to await my return.

The guest bathroom was at the far end of a long, dimly lit hallway. While I was in that end of the house I passed a dark, unused bedroom. I went inside and unlocked the sliding glass door that opened directly onto an outside patio. Then I was gone.

"This is the gate," I said, back at the Wonderland house, retracing the lines on a hastily drawn diagram with my finger. "Jump over it - don't open it - and take the path that leads around to the back of the house. And here..." - I choked momentarily on the words; my throat and lips were suddenly bone dry - "...is the door to the back bedroom. Just slide it open and go inside."

My head throbbed. My body trembled with fear. No longer was I the gofer, running goods and messages between battlefields. I had willingly, spitefully, become an integral part of the plan. The floor felt like quicksand. With each move I could feel myself sinking deeper and deeper.

"Where's our stuff? Where's he stashing it?" Billy wanted to know. His words were slurred. He looked a mess.

"How the fuck do I know?" I answered, testily. "You wanted me to find a way to get you inside - and I did. Want me to go over it again?"

I looked into the faces of Billy, Ronny, Karl and a young man they called Apache Kid, who'd been brought in as their driver. (Apache kid owed Wonderland a great deal of money; he had been told that he could pay off his debt, and make a few bucks as well, if he'd come in on the Nash job.) The four men were staring blankly, as if I'd just spoken to them in some foreign tongue.

"Two things," I said quickly. "Remember to break the glass and rip the screen on the sliding door to make it look like you broke in. I don't want to be tied into this. And no rough stuff. No one gets hurt. Understand?"

Did I really believe that these people had heard a word I'd said? Or that they'd try to avoid a shoot-out? They were addicts, desperate and violent. Any one of them would have killed their own mother if she had gold in her teeth.

The fact is I wanted to believe that they could pull it off without any problems. In my own mixed-up mind, my future was at stake. The success of this job would be my ticket out. Once it was over, I'd never get involved again. Or so I kept telling myself.

"Something's wrong," Barbara said in a low voice. "Why are they taking so long?"

"Quit bitching," Joy moaned. "I'm sick enough without listening to you." She made a move for the television remote, then pulled back. She didn't have the strength; she'd been throwing up all morning.

It was nearly 9:30 A.M.; the men had left for Nash's shortly after 8:00. Barbara had reason to be concerned. If things had gone smoothly, they should have been back before 9:00.

A half-hour later, we heard the sound of screeching tires outside as a car roared to a stop. "We did it! We did it!" Ronny hollered as the men raced through the front door and upstairs into one of the bedrooms. They each carried huge plastic bags filled to overflowing.

By the time Joy, Barbara and I joined them; the bags had been emptied on the bed. It looked like they'd cleaned Nash out. There were bundles of money, pouches of cocaine and heroin, bags of jewelry and precious gems, wristwatches, cameras - and the guns. Over a quarter of a million dollars in cash and loot!

"Did you cut the screen and break the glass?" I asked uneasily.

Ronny, Karl and Apache Kid were too busy congratulating themselves to answer. Billy was on the phone calling every drug dealer in town. "We just knocked over that little Arab fart," he shouted, "tied him up and told him he was maggot meat unless he handed everything over to us. You should have heard him whimper. He begged us not to hurt him."

What the hell was going on? "Ronny, the sliding glass door!" I repeated. **"Did you break it?"**

Ronny ignored me. He was tuned into Billy, listening to the sordid retelling of the past few hours, and he was cracking up with laughter.

"Yeah, the little squirt got down on his knees and begged us," Billy went on. "We should have shot him instead of that tub of black shit. Sure, we shot Diles - left him in a heap on the floor!"

Jesus Christ!

I couldn't believe what I was hearing. The worst had happened, the absolute worst thing possible, and Billy was letting the world in on it. (Nowhere does news travel faster than in the drug world.) He might as well have called in the reporters. I felt sick.

The story was told and retold, each time with more bizarre embellishments, before Joy finally yanked the phone out of Billy's hand. It wasn't his uncontrolled yapping that had her at his throat; she was used to that. Rather, she was desperate for her split of the heroin. The loot, all of it, was to be divided into unequal shares, the bulk going to the original members: Billy, Ronny and Joy.

No mention was made of Sam or the $125,000 they owed him. Screw Sam! Screw Nash! Screw the world!

While the haul was being divided up, the room was chaotic. Everyone was shooting drugs and scurrying around, yanking clothes from the drawers and hangers, and wildly stuffing them into open suitcases. Billy and Ronny made calls to the airlines in a frantic attempt to arrange out-of-town flights for the following morning. They were so stoned, and totally disorganized, that leaving that day never came up. Billy and Joy were heading for Hawaii; Ronny and Susan were going back to Sacramento. Karl and Barbara were already half out the door to some unknown address in Pasadena.

I was going nowhere fast, and the thought had me in a cold sweat. The heist had turned into a monumental fuck up. It didn't take a lot of brains to know that my ass was in the wringer. No, my life was on the line. Nash <u>had</u> to know of my involvement. And after the stupid phone calls, it wouldn't take Sam long to make the tie-in. I had to get away too, if not out of the city then away from Wonderland.

John Holmes......hands on promotion of VCA videos in 1983.

John, 8 years old, holding half-brother David.

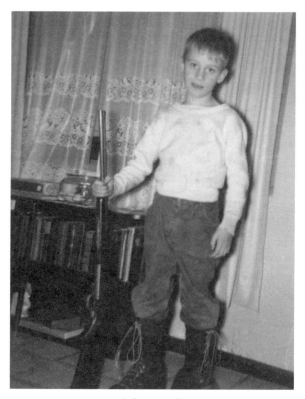

John, age 7

John, age 10, with his new pup in Ohio.

John, age 10, and his older brother Eddie.

*Promotion photo for
VCX "Dreams of Misty"
Misty Dawn, 1984,
age 21*

*Just hangin, by Palm
Springs Tram*

John loved to go fishing off the Channel Islands, summer 1983.

Misty Dawn, 1983, age 20 in Bill Amerson's back yard.

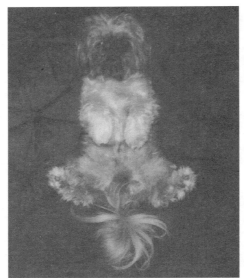

Our dog "Charlie". He fit right into the family.

With all that was going on in his life, John took as much time as he could to "find places to bury treasures" in the outdoors.

John and Laurie (young Misty) 1983.

Palm Springs
"Get the Message?"

John and Laurie (Misty Dawn) wedding picture,
January 24, 1987, fourteen months before John's death.

John and Laurie "getting into their rolls." Knotts Berry Farm, 1984.

The "real" John never left home without his machetti!

Promotional photo of Misty Dawn, age 22.

John always had a line clear out the door for his autographs, VSDA Convention, 1983.

John at the Consumer Electronics Show, Las Vegas, 1984.

Making it on Broadway: the FIRST adult film to be advertised on a billboard in Times Square.(1984)

*Naked City, Indiana. Nudest Colony where John judged Miss Nude
USA contest. John always enjoyed his fans.*

*Always looking for a good ride!. . . and
like his machetti, he loved a good chopper.*

Young John, mid-20's "actor photo" to be passed around Hollywood agents.

John often practiced yoga – why not nude?
Can you achieve this pose?

John, Ginger Lynn and VCX Executives in 1984

Publicity still for "Girls on Fire," 1984, with Ginger Lynn.

Young "Stud" John

The Johnny Wadd films paved the way for on-location shooting.

"John C. Holmes dares you to sit through the most erotic film he's ever made. . . LIQUID LIPS"

Publicity still for "The Jade Pussycat," 1973, with Linda Wong.

John's return to films after an absence of nearly two years.

*A night for porn to really shine along with the KING.
In 1984, during the preview of "Girls On Fire" John was
immortalized (with signature and hand prints) in front of the
Hollywood Pussycat Theater.*

John – just making the best out of the worst. A definite challenge for a real man!

CHAPTER 8

Brandy and I had been involved in a lengthy, torrid relationship during the late 1970's. The hot times were over, but we'd remained friends. I'd started calling Brandy and other old girlfriends shortly after I became a fixture at Wonderland, especially at night when the house rocked with strangers and blaring music. Time alone, or with no more than one other person, has always been important to me. I'd screwed up my life, but I still cherished moments of peace and privacy now and then.

The calls had resulted in invitations to come over, and I'd stay for a night or two. Perhaps these ladies expected more from me than I could deliver; if not the old flame, then certainly a pilot light. Since I'd buried myself in drugs, no one could get a rise out of me. Brandy didn't mind. That is, she didn't complain and she made no demands. Her only request was that I come to her whenever I grew restless at Wonderland. The door to her apartment in West Los Angeles was always open to me; she made no secret of that. She seemed content just to have me back, hanging around, sharing her bed. Remembering how much Brandy craved sex made me feel a little guilty. Had I been into bondage, she would have made the perfect slave; she gave so completely of herself. Nothing pleased Brandy more than pleasing her partner. No matter what, no matter who.

After fleeing the Wonderland house, I turned in desperation to Brandy. She was staying with her girlfriend in a small apartment. That's where I picked her up, and without a word of explanation - and no questions asked - we checked into a motel on Wilshire Boulevard near Santa Monica as Mr. and Mrs. Black. The accommodations weren't much, a hole-in-the-wall room and bath furnished in 1940's California "modern," but neither were the rates. Aside from that, the location was good. Across the street was a supermarket, open all night. Less than a mile away, on the other side of the Veteran's Administration property, was the San Diego freeway and a fast exit out of town, if necessary.

The motel was a change of scenery and little else. I could not escape the sound of Nash's voice or the penetrating stare of his eyes; he was with me constantly. Was I to disappear for the rest of my life - with images of Nash haunting me - or try to clear my conscience? Suddenly, I felt compelled to talk with Nash, to let him know that, despite what happened, I tried to keep him from getting hurt. Above all, I didn't want him blaming me. Or coming after me. In the past, whenever Nash had problems with anyone, he'd ask me to "grab a piece" and come help him save his life. Now there was no mention of trouble. "Everything's fine," he said, lightly. "Come on up."

Everything's fine? After he'd been tied, beaten and robbed? I knew he was aware of my involvement - yet he said nothing. For five minutes, we played word games over the phone. He'd invite me to "come on up" and I'd be noncommittal. Finally, he insisted. I couldn't refuse, nor did I want to. If I were to save my life, I had to plead my case.

Nash met me at his front door, not with a greeting, but with the butt end of a .357 across my face, splitting open my lower lip. Blood oozed down the front of my shirt as he smiled.

His look was chilling and evil.

I stood in Nash's doorway, momentarily reeling. The blow caught me by surprise, but I didn't lose my senses. "You said you'd back me up and you didn't," I lashed out. "I tried to warn you three times. Three times! People were going to be killed, and I didn't want that. I had to do something!"

Nash waved the pistol in my face. As I backed away, two of his bodyguards grabbed me. Diles appeared from nowhere, looking fit as ever. He taped my wrists behind me. I was dragged into the living room, dropped into a chair, and held at gunpoint.

"Don't bother to explain, you asshole," Nash hissed. "Those fucking friends of yours told me everything."

"They're not my friends. They're scum!"

"Scum - like you! You set me up!"

"I didn't want..."

"Shut up!" he shrieked, flapping his arms wildly. Suddenly, he dropped to his knees, cowering as he looked up at me. His eyes overflowed with tears and great gobs of saliva dangled from his open mouth. He cried uncontrollably for several moments before turning savage again. Leaping to his feet he began pacing like a panther in a cage waiting for the meat to be tossed in. At one point, he hurled a large cut-crystal bull, worth many thousands of dollars, in my direction, smashing at my feet. I'd been around my stepfather when he had his raging fits. I'd seen heroin junkies at their worst - swinging in behavior from supreme arrogance to sniveling low-life without warning. But I had never seen anything like this.

He stood before me, so close that I could feel his foul breath against my face. "Did you know your friends were shooting up while they were here?" His voice was low now, barely audible, as he growled out the words. "Did you know they were shooting my stuff, taking turns going into the back bedroom...the room with the unlocked glass door?"

"The door?" I repeated, unconvincingly.

"Don't give me that shit!" he blared, storming about the room again. "I know what you did. Your friends told me everything!"

"Nothing would have happened if you'd kept your word."

"Did you know they forced me to the floor and made me beg for my life..."

"I saved your fucking life!"

"....and how they shot at Diles? The pricks would have killed him if they hadn't been so wired." Nash stopped in his tracks and raised his arm in Diles direction. "Show him, show him!" he barked at the big black man. "Show this turd where they hit you."

Diles kept the gun trained on me while he lifted his shirt with his free hand. I saw no sign of a wound, only traces of powder burns along one side just above his waist.

"I thought he was dead!" Nash screeched. "They tried to murder him. They humiliated me. They ripped me off!"

"I brought some of the stuff back," I said. "My split to prove to you that...."

"What? Where?" He said quickly, cutting me off.

"Outside...in my car."

Diles tore the tape from my wrists and shoved me out onto the driveway. As I climbed into the car to retrieve Nash's goods, I noticed his small hand reach for something in the front seat. It was my address book containing the names of every person I knew in the whole world: friends, relatives, business acquaintances. "That's mine, dammit!" I said.

"Nothing is yours anymore," Nash snarled.

Diles led me back into the house, and for the next eighteen hours I sat with a gun pointed to my face. From one of the other rooms, I could hear Nash on the phone. He was making call after call in French, Arabic, English - he spoke six or seven languages - to girlfriends, customers and business associates, telling that he was holding John Holmes captive and all while inviting them to "come on up" to see his latest prize.

What was it with these people, I wondered, that they had to spout off like giddy teenagers after a hot date? Why couldn't they keep their mouths shut?

Shifts of bodyguards took turns watching over me, threatening to pull the trigger no matter how still I remained. My life was over; they made that very clear. I would not live to see the sunrise. My body would disappear in the muck of the Torrance oil fields, never to be found.

I had every reason to believe them, but as the hours passed I began to doubt that Nash would have me killed in his own house. Too many people were wandering in and out to ogle "the double-crossing porn prick" and hear the lowdown on my despicable deed. Every one of them was a witness to my being at Nash's house.

Around 2:00 A.M. I was left alone with my bodyguard. For the next few hours, I didn't see another soul; the house seemed deserted except for the two of us. Then, as the sky was beginning to brighten, Nash and his cronies calmly emerged from his bedroom with a gun in his hand. "Take this," he said, handing it to me, "and go over to Wonderland. If you get the rest of my stuff back I'll forget what happened.

The proposal was insane. Wonderland was an armed camp. No way could one person do what he was asking. Perhaps that was Nash's reasoning too. It sounded like he was setting me up. By letting the Wonderland people kill me, his hands would be clean.

I had to go if only to get out from under his thumb. Once away from Nash and back at Wonderland, I'd warn everyone then scramble over the hill. I even considered going to the police.

The gun scared the hell out of me; I didn't want any part of it. "This gun's no good," I told Nash, fumbling for an alibi.

"What do you mean no good? Hold it up to your temple, wise ass, and pull the trigger. You'll see how good it is."

"It doesn't have a silencer."

"Yeah? So what?"

"What about the neighbors? They're all around that house. They'll hear the shots."

He looked about to explode. Then he did. "We don't have a gun with a silencer," he shrieked. "Just kill them the best you can!" As he handed the gun back to me, he added, "And to make sure you've done the job, I want to see everyone's eyeballs. Take a baggy with you and fill it with their eyeballs."

Two cars filled with Nash's hit men followed me to the Wonderland turnoff, then parked near a school while I continued on.

The house at 8763 was dark and strangely quiet - no sounds of voices or hard rock coming from within. It didn't seem likely that everyone would be asleep. They'd just scored a tremendous amount of money and drugs. There should have been one hell of a party going on.

The front gate was wide open. That was odd. I walked through then clicked the latch, but not before one of the pit bulls darted by, brushing my leg and yipping pathetically. I called out, but it kept running. The other dog was nowhere to be found.

I made my way along the walkway to the front door and knocked. When no one answered, I knocked again, repeatedly. The door remained shut. If I'd had a key I would have used it, but no one had a key to the house. There was no need for keys, I'd been told. Someone was always home.

From the first day I set foot in the house and became part of the family, Joy and Billy had stressed the importance of keeping all the doors and windows locked and bolted. There were no exceptions, no excuses. The thought of unsuspecting strangers, or worse, wandering inside had them paranoid with fear. It was that unrelenting fear that led them to buy the two pit bulls.

Another entrance to the house was located on the backside. I walked around and started pounding. As my knuckles landed, the door cracked open. Bad enough that it wasn't locked. Someone had neglected to shut it tightly. Joy would hear about that!

A rush of foul smelling, warm air greeted me as I started

inside. I'd become accustom to Wonderland's stagnant air, even the occasional stench of garbage and unbathed bodies. But this was different, worse than I'd remembered. It was as if all the toilets in the house had backed up. Defying Joy's warnings, I purposely left the door open.

Where was she? I wondered. Where were Billy and Ronny, and the others? *Someone* had to be in the house. Unless they'd changed plans since I'd last seen them, they hadn't talked about skipping town until later in the morning. I figured that they'd slammed heroin all night and were lying in a stupor somewhere.

Near the downstairs bedroom, which I'd often used, I stepped on something soft. As I kicked it aside I noticed that it was one of Joy's old housecoats. It hit the wall, leaving a long red smear, before falling again to the floor.

The bedroom door was spattered with red. I reached out to touch it, then stopped short. I didn't have to get any closer to know that it was blood.

A trail of blood led from the door into the room. One wall was splashed with the sticky substance as it formed an icicle pattern on the plaster. Not far away, a long shape sprawled across crumpled, blood-soaked sheets. It was difficult to see in the dim morning light, but it appeared to be a body - a body without a face. Its head had been split open, pulverized into mush and drenched with blood. But the hair, the clothes...

God, it was Ronny!

My heart pounded as I ran back out into the hall, stumbling over the bloodstained clutter that lay scattered across the floor.

Joy...Billy. Where were they?

I made for the stairs, taking them two at a time. My legs felt wobbly. I was certain my knees would buckle at any time.

Light-headed, I stood hanging onto the rail at the top of

the stairs, straining for air. The heat was unbearable. And the stench! If anything, it had grown stronger.

The silence was deafening. I strained to hear sounds of life, but I heard nothing. Only the rush of blood - <u>my</u> blood - pulsating through my head.

I turned slowly to face Joy's room. The door was open, but it was dark inside. Even so, I could see the ugly stains on the carpet, and the huddled shape of another body.

It was lying in a heap, not ten feet away, twisted and grotesque like a battered rag doll. I didn't want to look but I couldn't stop myself.

The rumpled housecoat and matted, reddish hair were the only remaining identifying features. Joy's head, what was left of it, looked like someone had run it through a shredder.

Across the room, Billy's lifeless form lay motionless on the floor. A gooey mess was oozing from the remnants of his open skull. His brains had literally exploded.

How many devastating blows with a heavy object, such as a club or lead pipe, does it take to rip open a human skull? One...two...three, at the most. The person - or persons - responsible for these heinous murders hadn't stopped there. Joy, Billy and Ronny had been struck forty or fifty times each. Maybe more. Their heads were mutilated. Pulverized. Nothing remained but slime.

A crazy person had to have done this. A nonhuman. Someone consumed with unrelenting anger. The room was filled with anger. And blood. A vampire could have gorged for days on the drippings.

Blood was everywhere, soaking the carpet and bedding, splattering the walls and furniture, staining the ceiling. It was as if an insane animal had sloshed buckets of blood over everything in sight. I was standing in a slaughterhouse. Or in a mad room, trapped in another dimension.

The smell of blood and human waste was overpowering. Nothing in the world smells like violent death. I'd scraped bodies off the freeways when I had worked for an ambulance company. I'd picked up dismembered hands and arms and legs, but this was a hundred times worse. I can still smell it.

I can still feel the anger.

Was my mind playing tricks on me? Was this a cruel hoax or just another setting for a grisly film fantasy? <u>It's Johnny Wadd - back in action!</u> But where were the other actors, the cameras, the lights? Where was the director? Why wasn't he hollering, "Great shot! That's a wrap?"

I felt like puking, but I couldn't. I couldn't do much of anything except wander about in a daze. My brain wasn't functioning normally. I couldn't see straight; my ears thumped with the sound of my own heartbeat. Run away? I hadn't the strength. Go to the police? Not with three people dead.

In my stupor I thought only of clearing myself with Nash, making him believe that I had carried out his orders by bringing <u>something</u> back to him.

I began searching frantically through the bloody mess. The suitcases that had been so hurriedly packed after the burglary were now on the floor, open and empty, along with the discarded contents of closets and drawers. Lamps, clocks, magazines and clutter had been swept from tabletops and flung about like leaves in a violent windstorm.

Less than 24-hours before, the bed had been piled high with Nash's riches. Now it was stripped bare. Even the mattress had been searched and left hanging limply over the bloodstained box spring.

Joy had always kept her good jewelry secretly hidden in a shoe box. Someone had known where to find it. The box was on the floor; its contents scattered and smeared with red. I pawed through the sticky strands but could find nothing of value. I scooped it all up, dumped it back in the box, and took it anyway.

On the carpet, half submerged in a small circle of coagulated blood, a solitary eyeball stared up at me. It was there for the picking. I felt a tightening in my stomach, and I turned away.

The other rooms in the house, upstairs and down had been ransacked as well. Every drawer was empty, every shelf swept clean. Nash's coveted possessions had vanished. The guns that earlier rested within arm's reach on every flat surface were gone. So was Ronny's knife collection. I hurriedly retraced my steps, stumbling over tossed debris in the eerie light, and grabbed what I could, all of it worthless.

What possessed me to wander through that horrifying house of death, knowing that the killer - or killers - might still be there, lurking around the corner or in the next room? I can't honestly say. I only know that something was pulling at me, compelling me to go on. Perhaps I felt threatened by Nash's men; I knew they were outside in their cars, waiting for me. As it turned out, they weren't.

My hands pressed uneasily on the car horn, sending out a sharp sound that shattered the early morning stillness. Slowly, Nash's garage door opened and I backed the car inside.

Nash was waiting there for me. "You came back," he said, suspiciously.

"Of course I came back," I replied. "Why wouldn't I?" I tried to sound as positive as possible, under the circumstances, as though everything had gone as planned.

If Nash noticed the uncertainty in my voice, he didn't let on. "Where's my money?" He asked, changing the subject. "Where's my coke?"

I opened the car trunk and pulled everything out: crumpled clothes, paste jewelry, boxes of used drug paraphernalia. "This is all that was there," I said, pointing to the pile of junk.

Nash pawed through the stained odds and ends. "So much blood", he smiled, wiping his fingers. "You could have been neater."

"I wasn't trying to be neat."

"And this is it? You got everything?"

"Everything."

"Well, that's O.K.," he said, with a toss of his head. "The important thing is you did it. You really did it!" He began jumping up and down, clapping his hands together, and shouting, "Good! Good!"

That's O.K.? Good? Good? As welcome as those words were, I couldn't believe that Nash was accepting my return - and the worthless delivery - as a fait accompli. Why wasn't he more concerned about his stolen property? The man had lost enough cash and merchandise to buy 100 new Cadillacs. Why wasn't he rummaging through my car to make sure I wasn't holding out on him? Why wasn't he demanding to see the baggie?

"Take this crap and dump it where no one will find it," he told one of his men. "You know where." Nash had a favorite dumping ground in the ghetto of Los Angeles. "Those cops never poke through the trash cans in that area," he once confided to me, "and black people never turn shit in."

For the next hour, Nash kept me by his side, congratulating me on a job well done. He put on quite a show. He almost had me believing that he'd bought my story. Almost. I couldn't shake the feeling that something was crazy. Nash was much too intelligent to be conned so easily. He had to know more than he was letting on. Could it be that he - or his goons - had beaten me to Wonderland?

I began to blame Nash for everything. He detested the Wonderland people and had, in fact, threatened to kill them during one of his uncontrollable rantings. The humiliation he'd suffered at the hands of Billy, Ronny and Karl incensed him far more than the loss of his merchandise. He could always get that back, he said. But he could never regain his lost pride after they'd forced him to his knees to beg for his life.

It made absolute sense that Nash was responsible for the massacre. He and his bodyguards certainly had the time to hit Wonderland sometime after midnight when his house had seemed so strangely deserted for hours. He'd wanted me to believe that everyone was scoring in the back room. Yet no noise came from that end of the house. People on freebase make noise. They turn up the stereo full blast. They stumble into things.

All signs pointed to Nash - until I began to think about "Killer Karl". He was supposed to have gone to Pasadena with his girl friend - Susan Launius. Susan was the only survivor. I never saw Susan while rummaging through the house. "Killer Karl" knew the house was loaded with cash and cocaine. He'd kill anyone for a gram of coke, and there were bags of it at Wonderland. He could have taken all the loot for himself and split. Who ever did this made damn sure those people were dead.

And what about Sam? What if he had made good in his threat to knock over Wonderland? Time *had* run out.

Shortly before noon, Nash told me I was free to go. As I hurried for the door he held out a one hundred-dollar bill. "Call me," he said. "Keep in touch." Somehow I made it outside to the car.

I didn't know where to turn. My first thought was of Brandy, but I found myself heading for Sharon. Even though we'd been separated for years, and we hadn't talked to each other in months, I had to see Sharon again.

I stood nervously on her porch, my finger pressing hard on the bell. Then the door opened and she was standing there, staring at me with her arms crossed against her chest.

"Well?" she said, coolly.

It wasn't the greatest welcome but at least she was speaking to me. I doubt if her attitude would have been any different had I arrived nicely dressed bearing flowers. But here I was covered with blood, looking like a truck had just hit me. She didn't seem to notice my appearance, even my scraggly beard, mustache and long hair. It was my presence that called for an explanation.

"Well?" She repeated.

I was still half-dazed; words didn't come easily. "I've had...uh...an accident," I sputtered. "Can I...come in?"

Without saying a word, Sharon stepped aside. As I headed straight for the bathroom, I could hear her footsteps behind me. "I need to get cleaned up," I said, switching on the bathroom light. "Fill the tub for me...will you?"

I knew she heard me, but she didn't move toward the tub. Instead, she opened the medicine cabinet, pulled out some iodine and cotton swabs, and began dabbing at the blood on my face. She stopped after only a few seconds. I could tell by the expression on her face that she knew something was up. Being a nurse, she knew where to look and what to look for. But she saw only blood, no cuts or scratches. It was obvious the blood wasn't mine.

"You were in an accident?" she asked, almost accusingly. Not getting a response, she turned and started running water into the bathtub. It wasn't until the tub had been filled and I had submerged myself that she spoke again. This time she wanted to know exactly what had really happened.

How could I tell Sharon what I had seen only hours earlier? How could I relive that nightmare? But I had to tell her something and this time only the truth would do. I couldn't possibly make up a story as bizarre, or as sick, as the real one. "The murders," I said. "I saw what happened."

Sharon backed off slightly, a puzzled look on her face. Perhaps it was too soon for news of the murders to have been made public. Perhaps she hadn't even heard about what had taken place in the Wonderland house.

"I found all those people…and they were dead," I said, my voice starting to break. A rush of emotion had suddenly swept over me.

Sharon shook her head. "What are you talking about?"

"It was my fault," I replied, staring blankly ahead. "If I hadn't left the door open, none of this would have happened. They'd all be alive."

"Who? What?"

I told Sharon everything, the whole story from the setup to the robbery to the murders. And when I was done, all she could say was, "John, how could you?"

I don't know what I expected her reaction to be, but it was more than that. It didn't take me long to dress and make my way to the car. This time I headed straight for Brandy. Thank God she was still at the motel.

I was really dragging as she let me in. The hot bath plus the horrific events of the past twenty-four hours had really taken a toll on me. I felt weak, almost as if I was sleepwalking. I aimed for the bed without filling Brandy in on where I'd been or what had happened. I hadn't intended to nod off, but I did. Sleep, the great escape.

When I opened my eyes again, Brandy was propped in front of the television set, straining to hear; she had purposely turned the sound low so as not to disturb me. I felt awful, punchy and still a little queasy. As I turned over, trying to get more comfortable, the bed squeaked. Brandy was sitting beside me on the bed. She didn't look so hot either. From her expression I could tell the shit had hit the fan. Or, in this case, the news. "Something awful has happened at Wonderland," she said in a trembly voice. "You've got to see. They're showing pictures and everything."

I asked Brandy to turn up the sound, then run across the street for a newspaper. The images on the television screen sent chills through me. Cameras were positioned outside the Wonderland house, trained on the front door, as grim-faced police and plainclothes detectives moved quickly in and out. The coroner was seen briefly as he accompanied several shrouded stretchers, with the lifeless loads, beyond the yellow tape that cordoned off the house and out to the street where they disappeared in the crowd of stunned on-lookers. Not since the Manson murders, gasped an on-the-spot newscaster, had there been such a brutal massacre.

Watching the television screen was like reliving the night-mare. I could handle that, but I wasn't prepared for some of the details being broadcast. In the downstairs bedroom, one reporter noted, two battered bodies had been discov-ered. In the living room yet another. *He talked of five victims. I had combed the house from top to bottom and had found only three.*

When Brandy returned, she was carrying a box of Van de Kamp's donuts and two Special Edition newspapers, both headlining the killings. One of the papers had already put a tag on the bloodbath, calling it the "Four on the floor - Laurel Canyon Murders."

Every hour, it seemed, brought new information. The corpse in the living room had been identified as Barbara Richardson. The other victim was Susan Launius. She, too, had been bludgeoned, but she somehow managed to escape death after drifting in and out of consciousness for hours. If Barbara was at Wonderland then chances are "Killer Karl" was too! If "Killer Karl" was there, why wasn't he killed? Why was Susan the only survivor? The three bodies I had seen were brutally mangled - someone made damn sure they were dead - why didn't they make sure that Susan was dead too?

It was the discovery of Susan's lifeless body that had me completely mystified. In my fright, I could easily have over-looked Barbara on the dim and shadowy living room floor. But Susan and Ronny were reportedly found together. NOTHING MADE SENSE!

For two day's, I sat riveted before the television set listening to the latest developments. On the third day, I phoned one of my drug connections. The first words out of his mouth were: "The police have been by here looking for you - something about the Laurel Canyon murders."

"Why me?" I said, indignantly. "Why would they be looking for me?"

"The word is that over 160 informers have called in with information. They're talking to everyone who knows anything about what went on in that house. On top of that, the whole place has been fingerprinted. They've come up with a slew of prints, but only a half dozen or so have been identified. One of the sets was on the bed where Joy Miller was found."

I'd touched that bed. I'd touched almost everything in the house! "Tell me something I want to hear," I moaned.

"I'm telling you what I know," he said flatly.

I'd heard enough. Of all the people who had been in that house, the police were singling me out. Could it have anything to do with who I was? I wondered. Or had Nash implicated me?

One thing was certain: I couldn't stay in any one place too long without being spotted. Someone was sure to recognize me, or track me down. Brandy and I departed the Wilshire Motel within the hour.

We headed north on the San Diego freeway into the Valley, stopping briefly at Brandy's father's apartment in Burbank to pick up her dog. Our dog, actually. Brandy and I had raised Thor, a Chihuahua, from a pup while we were living together. When we'd split, her father agreed to take care of Thor for as long as necessary. Now Brandy wanted Thor back. "It'll be fun having us all together again," she said in a persuasive tone, trying to sell me on the idea. "Besides, he'll be good company." Anything to keep Brandy happy. Having Thor along did make us seem more like a family again, especially in the eyes of a Reseda motel manager, whose initial reaction to the arrival of "Mr. and Mrs. Black" was rather cool. He gave the impression that he was suspicious of all midday check-ins, particularly couples claiming to be married.

The temperature in the Valley was considerable warmer than on the other side of the mountain, and our tiny room was stifling, even with the door and window wide open. Several hours in the hot box was about all that I could take. I had to get outside, if only briefly. Either that or sweat away ten pounds, which I could ill afford. Brandy didn't want me to leave. "That's the dumbest thing I ever heard," she fussed, more concerned than angry. "Just stay put!"

"I've got to get some air," I replied, stubbornly. "And I'm out of cigarettes."

"John!"

"Hey, don't worry. I'll be back in a minute. I'll take the car."

"What if somebody recognizes you?"

I had to laugh. "Looking like this?" My cloths were a mess. My face was sprouting stubble; I hadn't been near a razor for four days. My hair was longer than usual, almost touching my shoulders. Sunglasses covered my eyes. People wouldn't stare; they'd turn away. They saw my kind on streets all over town. I'd turned into a common commodity, a California bum.

Wandering though the air-conditioned supermarket felt like a quick trip to Alaska. I could have stayed for hours, but that would have been pushing my luck, such as it was. A few minutes was really all that I needed to round up some bags of nibble food and cigarettes before returning to the motel.

Nearing the corner of Ventura Boulevard and White Oak, the signal changed. As I slowed to a stop, a car pulled up closely beside mine. Much too close! The driver didn't appear concerned; when I turned to look at him he was staring straight ahead. But in the back seat another man was growling at me through harrowed eyes. He held a revolver, pointing my way. It all happened in a split second: his finger squeezing the trigger, the burst of gunfire, the whoosh of hot air racing past my head, the shattering of glass. I floored the accelerator and sped through the red light, careening in and out of traffic until I reached the motel driveway. No one had followed me as I hurried inside.

Brandy nearly collapsed with fright when I told her what had happened, but she wasn't too weak to help pile furniture against the door to our room. The flimsy lock was useless; a strong breeze would have blown it away. Building the barricade was only a temporary solution at best. There weren't many options open to us: we had to get out of town, that much was certain. But where? After tossing around the names of several places, I came up with Montana. A distant cousin was living there. "Montana's perfect," Brandy nodded. "We could get lost in Montana." We decided to leave after sundown.

With the door and window closed, the room became a sweltering oven. I was so drenched with perspiration that my cloths clung to me as if they'd shrunk four sizes; I couldn't have been wetter if I'd fallen into a pool fully clothed and climbed out. One by one I began peeling off the sticky pieces until there wasn't a stitch left on me. Then I dropped spread eagle on the bed. Brandy disappeared into the bathroom to take a cold shower.

The running water must have drowned out the sound of approaching footsteps. I didn't hear a thing until huge hunks of splintered wood were flying about the room. I bolted upright in bed to face the barrels of four revolvers, two shotguns and a rifle poking through a gaping hole in the door. Behind them crouched seven uniformed bruisers with coat hanger shoulders, "Clark Kent" jaws and squinty eyes. I heard words like "freeze" (which sounded oddly appealing at the time) and "search him" (which didn't seem necessary, given my condition) as they crashed their way inside.

The officers dutifully went about their business - plundering the room - with strong-arm efficiency, casting sneerful glances and an occasional snide remark in my direction as they moved within grazing distance of my vulnerable front and backside. Only one of the men, the cop who read me my rights, showed any compassion. When he saw my starchy complexion, no doubt drained of its final bit of color by the surprise break-in, he commented, "You don't look so hot, Holmes. Are you sick?"

"Hell no," I snapped, "I've never felt better." Actually, I could understand his concern. In the dresser mirror, I caught a glimpse of myself. I looked like a vanilla popsicle, stick and all.

Brandy missed most of the fun, but not all of it. During the search, she was discovered in the bathroom and was told to dress. Then I climbed into my clothes. We were both handcuffed and put in a squad car, along with poor, frightened Thor. He'd been found under the bed, a quivering ball.

We were taken to Parker Center, the central police station in downtown Los Angeles where Brandy and Thor were released. I wasn't. They wanted me to talk about the Laurel Canyon murders. I said that I didn't know anything, which wasn't the information they wanted.

"Then we'll have to hold you," an officer said.

"On what charges?"

"How about the stolen typewriter?"

I couldn't believe he was bringing that up. The typewriter was piece of junk and it wasn't stolen. I'd found it in an alley next to a trash can when I was making a delivery in Santa Monica several months earlier. Thinking that I could fix it, and pawn it off, I'd stashed it in the trunk of my car. They'd found it during the search.

"The point is," the officer went on, "we want to keep you

in protective custody because we've received several reports about your death - one from Texas and another from Oklahoma. We have every reason to believe that someone is out to kill you."

"That's a damn good guess," I replied. "Let me tell you about bullet holes!"

The officer didn't press on. He made a phone call instead. Soon, I was on my way to L.A. County Jail.

Perhaps the sight of other prisoners crowded into dingy cells, surrounded by steel bars and cold concrete, was simply a ploy: a taste of things to come if I refused to cooperate. I only know that my stay didn't last the day. By late afternoon, I was being escorted to the parking lot where five unmarked black cars, each filled with cops, were lined up waiting. My escorts guided me into the middle car and we were off, slowly pulling away, one by one.

The procession wound its way through downtown Los Angeles until it reached the shiny glass cylindrical towers of the Bonaventure Hotel. Before I could set foot inside, however, four carloads of police swarmed the lobby to check for suspicious characters, a precaution that probably left the management and guests feeling somewhat shaky.

The police cordoned off an entire upper floor of one tower, and locked me alone in a room. I was advised to "stay put" and not to "try anything" because SWAT teams were not only occupying the rooms on either side of me but were on guard in the hall outside my door. Who would be the first to put the hit on me? I wondered, the police who were after a statement or some hired killer?

As it turned out, I wasn't alone long. My first visitor was a public defender, an outgoing young guy who'd be representing me on the stolen typewriter charge. Shortly after he left, Brandy was brought in - minus Thor; she'd taken him back to her father in the Valley. It was so good to see Brandy again, and to have her company. A couple of hours later,

Sharon showed up. The police had decided they needed protective custody too. The three of us sat talking and watching television all night, avoiding the heavy subject on all of our minds, figuring the room had to be bugged.

The next morning, I was transferred to a room in a really crummy hotel on the other side of downtown while Sharon and Brandy were released. One look at the place, and the surrounding crowd, and I knew that the "kid gloves" treatment was over. Dozens of people crammed the room. The FBI was there, along with members of the Food and Drug Administration, the LAPD and District Attorney's office, secretaries and stenographers - and they were all waiting for me to say something. I told them what I knew, which wasn't much, only to hear: "That's absolutely no help at all. We need you to tell us who did it. Who is responsible for the killings?"

"I can't tell you," I replied. "I honestly don't know?"

One of the officers stepped forward. "It comes down to this, Holmes," he said patiently. "You were a regular in the Wonderland house and someone is trying to kill you." He paused, his eyes studying me as he waited for a reaction. I nodded, feebly. "You're safe now," he went on. "Remember that. And you needn't have anything to fear in the future. We'll keep you hidden away somewhere under armed guard, and protect you until the trial comes up - in fact, until the killer's in jail - if you'll testify against that person, whoever it is. We happen to think you know." He paused again; this time he got no reaction. The officer moved a step closer and said in a low voice, "If you won't tell us who did it, we're just going to have to let you go. You'll be out on the street - and you'll be on your own. Just don't leave California."

The offer was appealing, but there was nothing I could tell the police that would satisfy them. I had no choice. I was going back on the street.

Knowing I was a marked man, I had to leave town. First, however, I had to get my hands on some money. I called

Nash; who gave me $150.00 on the spot and offered $500.00 more if I came back that night. I knew that Nash always kept a minimum of $10,000 in cash on hand, which made me very suspicious. I promised to return but instead I called my half-brother David. After all the years of supporting David, I felt it was time for some repayment. He came up with $50.

Desperate to get away, I dyed my hair and newly grown beard black, put an eye patch on and headed for Montana with Brandy. We spent three weeks in a small town but with a turn in the weather Brandy began to long for Florida, where her brother lived. With only three dollars in my pocket, we returned to California — narrowly escaping a highway patrol officer along the way — to raise money for the long, cross-country trip. Back in Los Angeles, I paid Nash an unexpected visit. He gave me $500 and told me, once again, to come back that night for more. Another invitation to death????

With the cash in hand, we quickly took to the road and headed for Florida. Believing that the police were tracking me, I bought some cans of spray paint and repainted my car at frequent intervals. I didn't know that the police had broadcast my license number to every small town, city and state across the country. Nor did I know that the FBI had contacted my family in Ohio, and had staked out the New York premiere of Exhausted, my last film prior to the murders, thinking I might show up. I had been put on the FBI's 10 most wanted list.

In Miami, Brandy and I checked into a sleazy motel that catered to traveling salesmen and prostitutes, convenient to the strip joints and bars across the road, where we both started working to pay expenses. I also moonlighted on a construction job, but my earnings couldn't even come close to covering a lofty repair bill on my car, which was being held behind locked gates at the garage awaiting payment. Apparently, the long trip had taken its toll on our car. Frustrated and feeling trapped, I plotted to break into the garage one night, steal my car and take off for the southern tip of Florida — without Brandy.

Several days later, after six weeks, in Miami, Brandy took off on her own, leaving me with ten dollars and the rent due. Her departure came as no surprise. She didn't say it but I knew that once she got to Florida she'd take off. Before I could get away, however, I was apprehended by two Los Angeles homicide policemen, taken to jail, then court. As it turned out, Brandy's brother had been arrested and with her information about my whereabouts, they released her brother. I did not fight extradition. Screw it, I hadn't done anything. I just wanted to go home and get it over with. I was tired of running!

My attorneys had based their strategy on my testimony, in spite of the fact that I refused to talk. They held me for the robbery charge in Santa Monica and I received a three-year probation. Then I was taken to court again on an unrelated drug case (the D.A. was grasping at straws). After all this, I thought it would all be over. Then I got subpoenaed before the Grand Jury, which was convinced that I still knew something about the murders. Although I had my suspicions, for me to say anything - suspicions or otherwise - would have put my family and friends in danger.

Once a week I was taken to court to hear the judge ask, "Are you going to testify?" My answer never varied: "No, your Honor, I cannot." They told me that I held the key to my own jail cell. All I had to do was testify and I could get out of jail, a free person. Fine, I thought to myself, but what is freedom if you are dead or you have to live with the guilt of someone you love dying because you got a big mouth?

At an interrogation in Los Angeles, I was given another ultimatum: "Tell who committed the murders or be charged with them - because we don't have any other suspects." I stuck to my story that I didn't know who was responsible. For that I was hit with four counts of murder. Not much later, the police called my mother. They put me on the phone with her in the belief that she could get me to talk. When she asked me if I wanted her to come out, I told her "No, the media will eat you alive. Stay away from me!" That was the last time I thought I would ever talk to my beloved mother again.

In court it was brought out that by pressing charges against me, it would put me in the position of having to talk. I remained silent. My suspicions meant nothing. And without proof I couldn't risk opening my mouth and involving hundreds of people. Nash still had my address book. If he was the one who was really responsible for the murders, and I told the events as I knew them, it could endanger the lives of my family and others. I didn't give a shit about being in jail! I remained quiet as a matter of honor, and a whole lot of fear.

I was incarcerated for 18 months in a cramped cell in the maximum-security section (called High Power) of the Los Angeles County Jail. I was miserable! Few visitors came, but I had a lot of time to think. It's times like that when you realize who your friends are - or for better choice of words, are not! The only visitors I had were my attorneys and the District Attorney, whom I believed had a vendetta against me, or so the papers reported. Could it be he was after "the most notorious porno animal in the world...?"

The trial seemed to drag on and on. At one point, a portion of a magazine interview I had done was read — the part where I described how I came to be offered my first adult film and my off-the-cuff remark, "Who do I have to kill?" It was actually brought out in court that I was willing to kill for money. It was simply a smart-ass joke!

As the months passed, I became very depressed. I had been found innocent yet I was imprisoned. I had pled the 5th Amendment, my constitutional right, and yet I was still in jail! Maybe they didn't think a "Porno Star/Drug Addict" had any rights. I had all but given up when I decided to go on a hunger strike. I dropped over 40 pounds. My teeth were starting to loosen, my hair was falling out, and my eyesight was beginning to fade. Never before had I ever had the "shakes" like that. I was taken to County General Hospital to be fed intravenously. When a doctor threatened to put a hose down my throat and feed me baby food, I began to have second thoughts about eating.

Three-day's later, back in High Power, I received a note from my former drug dealer, Eddie Nash. He had been found guilty of possessing cocaine for sale and was a prisoner in the same jail. "Do what you have to do," he wrote. "You've suffered enough. Say what you have to say to get out of there." Hearing from Nash made me feel that he wasn't responsible for the murders. I guess I'll never find out who was for sure, but I do know that I never want to see anyone that might have had anything to do with that massacre again.

I was out of jail at last, stone-broke with no place to go. As far as my plans for the future, I hadn't a clue. I figured no one would even want to talk to me, much less hire me. As far as my friends were concerned, I didn't think I had any. I did, however, have one place to go. After this whole ordeal, along with the horrendous images that haunted my mind, one might think I would never want to go near drugs again. Not so! I had to have something to erase the thoughts and the fear that never seemed to go away. I had done a lot of business over the years with an old pal of mine, someone I had known for many years. It was Bill that had turned me onto cocaine in the first place. For better or worse, he took me in and before long my drug debt to him was growing higher and higher. Being a producer, Bill had many connections in the porno business as well, and before I knew it, I was back on the set again. All the bad publicity I thought was going to hurt me actually revved up my career. Suddenly, I was more in demand than ever - and just as "high" too!

"What did I have to lose?" I asked myself...

CHAPTER 9

L ittle did I know I would meet the girl who would melt my heart and change its course forever? Her name was Misty (Laurie, for real) and I knew I had to have her from the moment I saw her. I also knew she wanted me too, in a bad way. With her big brown eyes and long brown hair she had a special look about her, one that set her apart from the other girls and made her seem strangely out of place on an X-rated movie set.

Misty had other attributes that weren't quite so obvious at first glance. In time, I discovered her tenacious side. It didn't take long, however, to find out how persuasive she could be with the producer. We were shooting a film called Fleshpond in San Francisco when the news came that I would be doing a scene with her that wasn't in the script. Through some quick manipulation, she trapped me into doing the scene. I was angry with her at first, but not as angry as some of the other girls on the set who, in their jealousy, accused Misty of ripping things off from their dressing room. I knew Misty wasn't guilty, but one of the girls needed an excuse to cut up her face. These girls were rougher than the ones Misty worked with in Los Angeles, and I honestly believe they were mad at Misty only because they thought I was. But so what. Misty didn't deserve what was about to happen to her. Her intentions were not bad, just mishandled. Seeing the way things were going, I found myself protecting Misty and telling the girls to leave her alone. Somehow, we got through it all. Misty even apologized for involving me in the situation, and when the shoot was finally over, I gave her my phone number. I knew she would call.

It was four or five days before I heard from Misty. In the meantime, I was having fun with everyone who wandered my way. As dog-ass skinny as I was, it seemed some things never changed. Girls were there for my picking. In spite of what some people might believe, I am very much attracted to women. It has been rumored that I am gay so I guess it's up to me to set the record straight. Sure, I have done a few gay films in my days, but that was out of necessity. I needed the money back then, and it wasn't all that pleasurable for me. I am not putting down what I did; I certainly don't have anything against it. Different strokes for different folks, as they say. What makes us all unique is our right to choose whatever or whomever. Where would we be, and especially, where would I be without the sexual revolution? The point is I love women, the younger the better as long as they are legal.

I could tell how much Misty wanted me. She began calling and asking about cocaine. She wanted some, she said. I knew she really didn't do drugs, but business was business. Later, she told me she was only buying from me so she could see me, then not wanting it for herself, she gave it to her friends. She even convinced a producer to use me in the film <u>California Valley Girls.</u>

One night, on Bill's birthday, I asked Misty and a friend of hers to come up to the house. While I was really beginning to feel something inside for Misty, I definitely didn't want to get hung up on anyone. What better way to get rid of that feeling than by giving her away as a gift to Bill? Without saying a word to Misty about my "surprise," she figured it all out. She definitely wasn't stupid, even if she pretended to be at times. From then on Misty had what she wanted all along: to spend the rest of my life with me.

Misty understood everything, and would do anything I asked of her without questions. Having been around the porn business, she could relate to my life as a male prostitute. I never realized how much until the time she went to Palos Verdes with me, pretending to be my Goddaughter. We were meeting a very wealthy older woman who liked to pay guys to line up and "gang bang" her while an audience of her friends watched. Misty stood on the sidelines, taking it all in, not saying a word. She understood.

At home, Bill had a bedroom and connecting bathroom that adjoined mine. When Misty moved into the big house, she kept all her stuff in her room, but she slept with me. We had two separate phone lines so that there would be no confusion or conflict with all the business that was coming our way. One night I handed Misty a mirror so she could do a line of coke. I couldn't believe it when she refused. That was the first time anyone had ever said no to me on that subject, especially in California. Misty's excuse was that coke made her feel funny and unable to talk, that's why the few times that she had bought from me she didn't use it herself. I didn't argue with her. I simply went into the bathroom and freebased alone for about five hours while she sat on the other side of the door wondering if I was ever going to come out. I thought a lot about what she had said and the truth was, the shit didn't make me feel all that great anymore either. Even though my mind was all screwed up, I knew I had to get clean if I were to have any future at all. More than anything, I wanted that future to include someone in my life. Misty had far more willpower than I did. She was good for me; I needed her.

The two weeks that followed were very ugly as I went cold turkey. In spite of the monster I know I was, Misty stuck by me the whole way, and when it was over, I was feeling healthier and more vibrant than I had felt in years. We began to have so much fun, and I believe she was feeling young again too. She had missed out on being a kid just as much as I had, so we were making up for lost time, doing all the things we seldom got to do while growing up. It also helped that we had some money and the time to do them. We had a wild, wonderful time going from one amusement park to another, seeing movies, soaking up the sun at the Biltmore Hotel in Palm Springs, gambling in Las Vegas, and taking long walks on the beach. No matter where we went we laughed and basically made spectacles out of ourselves. We didn't care. We were living again!

There was only one dark cloud in our beautiful blue sky. I still had one hell of a debt with Bill, and one afternoon he called me on it. One of his pals in the gay market decided that a gay film with John Holmes would make several million dollars. The money sounded great, more than enough to get me off the hook. And while I didn't jump at the suggestion, I knew I had to do it.

Leave it to Bill to run and tell Misty. She was shocked and couldn't wait to call me on it. It helped that she had a permissive nature. It helped even more when she heard I would be making a million dollars on the deal. Not long before the offer, I had asked Misty to marry me, hoping to be able to get enough money together so that we could get out and away from "porno." The truth is I knew I would never make a million dollars by doing the film; it was just a way to pay off an old debt. But I had to tell her something.

Because of my prior experience in a gay film, again because of money, I felt that there was only one way to get through it: I had to be "high." How could I tell Misty I was doing drugs again? She was so proud of me. She looked up to me. I was her "Daddy." Thank God. She believed in me so much that as time went on she wound up being my perfect alibi. The little money I made off the film, after Bill got the major share, was just enough to pay some of our bills for a few months. I told Misty that Bill and his pal had claimed they didn't make the money they had hoped for, so there was no million to be had. Although she was disappointed, she seemed satisfied to hear that. And knowing we did make something, she believed an effort had been made to pay me.

Misty would basically do anything I would tell her to do, even be quiet if I told her not to ask questions. Still, there were times when I had to make it appear that things were not quite as they seemed to be. If I learned anything from my dealing with Bill and his pals it was how much it bothered me not to be totally honest with Misty. In the past, the business had forced me to lead numerous double lives, especially with tricks. I once had four different apartments, four different cars, sets of jewelry and clothes. I was very skilled at subterfuge, but this was different because I really loved Misty. Nevertheless, if necessary, I knew I still had to create a story to cover my ass for anything that might come up in the future. It usually worked out fine in the past, and it did this time, too. Misty not only believed the money story; she began to resent Bill. From then on, she never believed anything he told her.

It was several weeks after finishing the gay film that I damn near died. I really don't remember much about this time except I was raging with fever and violent to the extreme, not at all myself, almost as if something foul had possessed me. If anyone set food before me I would throw it against the wall. My bedroom smelled of death for weeks. Finally, in a moment of weakness one evening, Misty was able to talk me into going to the hospital. That was fine until I overheard a nurse telling Misty she couldn't lie down with me. On hearing that I ripped out the IV and demanded Misty take me home immediately.

The next day Misty got me to go back to the hospital where she talked a nurse into readmitting me. Just in time, too. They were able to get enough fluid through the IV back in my body to cool my brain so it didn't fry. And while the doctors never told me what was happening, I knew. It was the drugs I had taken to get through the gay film. I had been clean for at least eight months before then, now my body was rejecting them. I was going through post "free-base blackout." My lungs, my brain, even my sense of existing were fried to hell, and it was all because of my stupidity. One would have thought I would have more sense considering the mess drugs had gotten me into before. This time, however, there was no snapping back. I got better, but since that episode I would never again be the real me, the real John Holmes.

Bill knew what was happening, of course, because he was my connection. He and I had an understanding about Misty; he knew better than to tell her I was doing drugs again. However, I later found out that he did try to tell her, but she didn't believe him. It was just as I had hoped where Misty was concerned. The "game" was working.

Yes, I was doing drugs again, but not as heavily as in the past and not all the time, as before. If I had learned anything from my earlier experience, it was that there was a time and a place for me to get high, and one definite wrong place and time was during the production of a film. I'm not making any excuses, but doing "chems" again became only an occasional thing following my illness. Most of the time I just smoked marijuana, and Misty joined with me in that.

Even though I was not feeling all that well, Bill told me it was time for Misty and me to get our own place. In other words, he was kicking us out. That was okay with me, he was charging us too much rent anyway. Misty soon found us an apartment in Encino. (It didn't matter that our "view" was the freeway directly behind the building.) She even went so far as to move most of our stuff all by herself. I could have probably helped her, but I was still very weak and she insisted she had the move under control.

Once we were settled in our new surroundings, I began to feel really badly about everything. Misty was such a trooper. She had endured so much from me, and yet she was still hanging in there at my side. I think if she'd have known the games I'd been playing, and involving her in, she would have run for any hill she could find. But to her credit, and my good fortune, she didn't. And luckily, for her sake and mine, not long after our move my health began to return. It was a lot easier for me, I guess, without Misty having to be around Bill so much.

The porno business, which had changed so much through the years, was really booming. We were an industry now, and a very big one, at that. Years before it was primarily films shown only on movie screens in random theaters, and before that it was sleazy middle-aged men selling grainy 8mm reels out of the trunks of their cars. Now porn was seen almost exclusively on video. Making videos was faster, more economical, and more profitable. It was also safer as far as racketeering was concerned. We could get hundreds of videos across the states instead of just one real of film to some unknown theatre. Video all but killed the theater business. Dozens of once thriving operations folded, leaving basically only one theatre chain still operating. That was because it was owned - and I do mean <u>owned</u> - by some very powerful people who needed the "front" for other matters.

Back in the 1970's, the business needed "stars" like Marilyn Chambers, Seka, a few others, and me. The thought behind the "star system" was to familiarize the public with a favorite performer, who would sell the product. Over the years, however, that reasoning began to change. The bigger the actors' head got, the bigger they wanted their paychecks to be, and it was far easier to get unknowns to work for less. Actually, the public really didn't care anymore. In fact, the appetite for new faces was greater than ever.

I was one of the lucky ones. Since I had more than a face to sell, the audience never seemed to tire watching me slam the meat to some young starlet. Call it an animal type of sex, if you will, but if worked for me. Besides, I was "in." Having achieved more than a slight degree of notoriety provided me the opportunity to take care of other matters when I had to travel somewhere without anyone else knowing, and still have an alibi for my time if it was something important. Since the Laurel Canyon episode, I had become a great money collector for other people. Although I didn't kill those people in the Wonderland house, no one was really sure of my innocence. Because of that, no one wanted to mess with me. So between my scenes, I could easily slip away without the wrong people knowing. They would just think I was resting in my company-paid hotel room, and since I had been escorted there, it wasn't a problem. I had it made. At night after filming, I was able to pick and choose among the cast to "play."

I had my favorite actresses; a few I even liked as friends. Ginger Lynn was the best around in the industry at this time.

I had a lot of respect for her. Ginger was different; she had class. Not only was she sweet and very sexy, she was, above all, a real person. I really liked her as a friend, not just another "girl toy."

Along with my favorites, I definitely had my dreads. During the filming of <u>California Valley Girls,</u> I got so pissed off at Kimberly Carson that I almost ran her down with my car. Most of the girls were nice, or at least had something positive going for them. If I didn't like someone, I'd try to forget why I didn't like her and focus on her one best feature. As pretty as a girl might be, if she were too much of a bitch for me to ignore, I would degrade her in my mind and make it as physically uncomfortable for her as I could. That may sound harsh, but that's the way it was. I called it "venge fucking."

Although I have worked with many blondes during my career, I have always preferred small, petite brunettes with dark eyes. I have found that most blonde, blue-eyed women have an attitude. They tend to act is if they are better than the other girls are, and so they don't try as hard. Brunettes give their all, and try even harder to please. Redheads are a lot of fun in bed, but they have the tendency of getting crazy if they become obsessed. It must be something in their genes. From my experience, there is no crazier woman than a red-headed one. As for wild women, I have to say Italians. They are the wildest, and nastiest, in bed. In fact, from my experience, bed is the only place they like to be.

If I learned anything about porno actresses over the years it's that the better the upbringing they had, the nastier they could be - and usually were. Throw in a few extra bucks, and a little attention, and a producer could get them to do just about any degrading, nasty thing he wanted them to do.

The same basic theory applied to women outside the business, as well. To me, it confirmed the old "preacher's daughter" theory. Usually, the preacher's daughter was the biggest slut in the church, town or wherever they happened to be. It seems that when standards are set too high for a person to live up to, then that person has more fun being bad. And there is no rebel like a horny one!

Drugs will definitely loosen up anyone. The things a person will never do straight will be done in a second once they're on drugs. Drugs and the business go hand in hand, anyway. From what I could see, most everyone in the business was on drugs, mostly cocaine, but we all had our favorites. How freely drugs were passed around on a set depended on whom you were working for. With some producers and directors drugs were a powerful way to control a situation, giving them an edge, perhaps getting a girl to do "favors" either for them or a friend. Most girls fall right into the trap, one they haven't a clue is being set for them. I have known very few actresses through the years who were smart enough to say no, especially if they thought it would get them closer to a person in power, such as someone who could land them future projects.

As for the male actors, the producers couldn't of cared less if they were high or not, as long as the guys could "get it up," and drugs definitely had an adverse effect in that area. During my worst drug burnouts, I was no better than any other male actor, except it was rather difficult to find a stand-in for me to "cheat the shot." Sometimes they would have to wait and wait, often being forced to go on to the next scene, then come back to me when I was ready. Of course this cost them time and money, but no one wanted to deal with me during a burnout anyway because I could be such an asshole. It was best to stay out of my face.

Bill had become a producer for one of the bigger companies, VCX, which meant I automatically had a job assisting in production and doing some directing. That was fine with me, except the added responsibility was little more of a cover for him when he either had to catch up on some sleep or snap out of a drug induced lethargy. Bill did have his good side, however, and in his own way he did take care of me at times. He knew I would back him up whenever necessary, even though I often disagreed with him. I guess anyone can have a good side, but it's too easy to get caught up in all the games we play. One thing that really annoyed me about Bill was that he never missed an opportunity to put me in a situation that brought him and Misty closer together. That happened way too many times.

It finally reached the point that I realized Misty would have to get out of the business. Having her around would have made it too easy for my enemies to get their hands on her, which would have put both of us in a dangerous position. There was another reason, as well. I didn't want Misty to find out I was doing chems again. I never wanted her to do drugs, and if she found out I was at it again, she would be more open to offers that would surely come her way. I knew that if I were to marry Misty, or even just love her, then there was only one solution: she had to drop out of sight.

How could I tell Misty she could no longer work? How could I force her to stay home and become a housewife? And how could I say she could not touch another man when for years I had lived off my wild "open sex" reputation? Not only was I proud of my notorious acclaim, I liked to fool around with other women. For me to tell Misty one thing and practice another would have me looking, and feeling, like a fool. I didn't believe in double standards. And while I knew that Misty would never want to be with another man, she was the type to go after what she wasn't supposed to have. Had I told her she could be with only me, she would have probably found herself with someone else. It didn't bother me for her to be with other girls. In fact, I encouraged her because, to me, that was different.

With Misty not being around people in the business, it made it easier for me to guide her into my way of thinking. It was only when Bill was around her that I had a problem. He put thoughts in her mind. But I had more power over Misty than Bill did, and it really began to get to him when his influence began to slip away. The seeds I had planted in her mind early on were taking root. And with Misty thinking a certain way, I could not only get out of whatever he might tell her, but I could turn those things back on him in her mind without him even knowing. In other words, the things he would say I was doing became the things he was doing, or so she believed. It worked beautifully. Misty always went along with Bill, even befriended him for telling her. She would then promise Bill that she wouldn't say anything to me, but she always did, giving me the edge over him. I later found out just how valuable she could really be to me in these matters.

By the end of 1984, the time had come for Bill and me to break away from our jobs and start making the big money for ourselves. Pornography was more popular than ever, taking in huge profits, so it seemed only natural for us to open our own company. Misty had become bored at home, and since we needed a girl to get us organized around the office, she seemed a good choice. Throwing her together again with Bill wasn't a big deal since her job wouldn't be lasting more than a few days. Little did I know just how good she would be. She surprised everyone, including Bill, who wanted her to work full-time. That didn't sit too well with me, but I agreed anyway. From my standpoint, there was one big advantage to having Misty around the office: who better to act as a spy for me? Bill, of course, was thinking the same thing, except he wanted her to be on his side. I tried to warn her that this "game" might become confusing, but she said she could handle it.

I knew that Misty was smart, but never in my wildest dreams did I ever think she would become the office manager, then go on to be the Vice President when we incorporated. The business part of it was easy for her, but I doubt if she fully realized that in her new role I would have to protect her more than ever. It was hard for Misty when people asked about her and I would say, "She is just my secretary," or even worse, "She is just my maid." I couldn't let on that we were involved, in fact, about to marry. For word to get out would not only pose a danger to her, it might mess up my "playtime."

"Why do you say those things about me?" Misty would ask, time and again. "Are you ashamed of me?"

"It's for your safety, Babydoll," I'd tell her. "I love you, but it has to be this way." That would be the end of it, until the next time. And while she went along with my excuses, feeble as they often were, she didn't like to hear me put her down, even jokingly. Of course my efforts were often vain. Bill seldom passed up an opportunity to tell some of his cronies about Misty and me.

Despite some run-ins with Bill, our business was moving along fine. Even the office was running smoothly, thanks to Misty. She had turned into a damn good bookkeeper, sometimes too good. There were occasions when she discovered discrepancies in the ledgers that made no sense to her. Coming to me for help, I had only to say, "What you don't know won't hurt you, girl." Her questioning ended there even though she once found me counting a floor full of money in our bathroom at home, money I had made doing a film - or so she thought. It was a lot of money, The whole entire bathroom floor blanketed with about ten inches of hundred dollar bills. I didn't want her to know about it because Bill and I already had plans for it, and those plans didn't include the company. So she wouldn't suspect anything, I put the money in my brown valise and took her out to lunch, telling her I'd be going to the bank afterward to put the money in a safety deposit box.

The money was really intended for two men who were sitting in the booth behind Misty and me at the restaurant. When we left, I "accidentally" left my valise on the seat. We were halfway to the bank when Misty discovered that I had left the money behind. Slamming on the brakes I made a quick U-turn and raced back to the restaurant, but it was too late. The valise was gone.

I had led Misty to believe that the valise also held my set of keys to the office, warehouse. Bill's house, our apartment and all the alarm keys too. Off to Bill's big house on the hill we went to tell him the bad news. He was standing in the driveway when we arrived. In on the scheme, he played along.

"A man just called, John," Bill told us. "He said he found your valise with keys and our business card inside."

"Thank God," I said. "Where did he find it?"

"Somewhere along Ventura Boulevard," answered Bill. "He was riding his bike when he spotted it."

Bill shrugged his shoulders. "No mention of any money."

There was no money in the valise, of course. But Misty always believed that some bus boy found it sitting on the seat where I had left it at the restaurant, and probably quit his job soon after. As far as Misty was concerned, the money was no more. The plan worked.

Our company was producing some pretty good flicks; the company was definitely in full swing. There was only one real concern on everyone's mind: AIDS. The AIDS epidemic was starting to hit hard, and although no one in the business had been reported as having it yet, we were all starting to get worried. Bill and I tried to organize an AIDS testing program within the business, along with some other people, including some screenwriters and still photographers. Our goal was to form an organization that would require current AIDS test results on every actor, male or female, we hired for a film. Everyone at our company, including me, got tested that year (1985), and our results all came back negative.

In discussion and on paper, testing sounded like a good idea, but when the time came to take action, the other performers surprisingly refused. No, they said, to testing, believing that to make it mandatory was in violation of their civil rights. There was also the matter of expense. An AIDS test was very costly at that time. For a disease that posed such a threat to our society, you would think the cost could have been a little more reasonable early on. To be brutally honest, I believe the way they handled it then was rather primitive. For example, it wasn't necessary to give the lab your real name so as to protect your identity in case your test came out HIV positive. I used the name "Karl Marx." Misty was "Betsy Ross," and Bill was "Jack Daniels." There was even talk about putting people with AIDS in the old Japanese internment camps to isolate them, much like lepers were at one time.

Misty wasn't making films anymore, but I was. Since we were unsuccessful in organizing AIDS testing within the business, I was still at risk, which meant Misty was at risk as well. Every time I made love to her we were taking a chance, but that was more on my mind than hers. As time went on, I found myself pulling away from her. We began to have stress all around us, within our private lives, and within the company, brought on by our daily head games. Stress or not, I was determined to make things work. All my life I had made money for other people and other companies. Now it was time to capitalize on my own name with my own company. I felt it would be my last chance of getting a large sum of money and breaking away from the business, which would make things easier at home.

Since the AIDS threat was hanging over my head, I somehow found it easier to play around. As terrible as it sounds, I really didn't care what happened to anyone else, but it would have killed me if I were to infect Misty with the virus. The Surgeon General was reporting that it takes four to sixteen weeks for the HIV antibody to show up in the blood system, so even if we had been successful in our efforts to organize AIDS testing among all the actors, the reports would not have been up-to-the-minute accurate. As it turned out, it was a good thing that I wasn't giving all my attention to Misty. One year after my first AIDS test, when I had tested negative, I decided to have another test. This time the results were not as good.

It was around February of 1986, not that many months following my first AIDS test, that I first felt my health slipping away. The earliest sign was an infection in my ears. Although I had seen my doctor about the bleeding, he passed it off as having been in the artillery while in the army. That made sense to me. But as the days passed I started getting a rash, not just any rash but one that would break out on the most visible - valuable - part of my body every time I had sex. If I had sex long enough after breaking out with the rash, I would bleed. Maybe it was that opening to my own blood system that caused me to catch the virus so easily. I guess I'll never know for sure.

As time went on, everything about my health began to get worse, prompting me to take another test. After finding out the deadly news, Misty had to be tested again too. While we weren't having a lot of sex during this period, we did get together just two weeks earlier. Her test came out negative, but we both knew it wouldn't be until after the second test months later that we would know for sure. That was a long couple of months for both of us. Thank God her second test was negative. Thank God I hadn't infected the love of my life.

It has been said that everyone has his or her time and destiny, and I can only believe that this was mine. "Why me?" Why was it, I wondered, that the most famous and successful porn star had to be the first person in the industry reported to have AIDS? There were many more actors and actresses doing much nastier things than I had been doing. It didn't make a whole lot of sense to me.

When I first got the devastating news, all I wanted to do was run away - from myself, from Misty and from the whole world. But I knew I would be able to keep the news hidden for only so long. So I stayed and waited for the other shoe to drop. And while I waited I began doing more and more drugs. What did I care? If I was going to die, and that was simply a matter of time according to my doctor, then I wanted to do everything I could to make it as quick as possible. I smoked eight packs of Marlboro's a day, and drank a lot more Scotch too. Drinking helped clear the phlegm from my throat, which made it easier to breathe, and alcohol helped to take the edge off the drugs. Misty and Bill kept trying to give me vitamins, but I never took them. A wasted motion, I convinced myself. At that point, I certainly wasn't interested in prolonging the inevitable.

It was nearly two months after my life-changing talk with my doctor that I was reminded it was time for me to make my annual appearance at the VSDA (Video Software Dealers Association) show in Las Vegas. I felt absolutely horrible, and I looked even worse. The banner above me read, "JOHN HOLMES, IN PERSON," but the letters should have spelled out, "JOHN HOLMES, THE WALKING CORPSE WHOSE HEART STILL BEATS!" I sure didn't want to show up in that condition, but I had to be there, not only for the company but to keep up appearances, such as they were. I was so self-conscious that I found myself repeatedly asking Misty if my makeup was all right. "You look fine," she'd say, adding a confident smile. Only then was I able to face the world and act as if everything was "hunky dory." In the past, I had looked forward to attending the four-day event. Now just the thought of being among all those people terrorized me. There were so many to greet, everyone I knew plus the thousands of fans who wanted autographs and pictures taken with me, some suggesting really wild, suggestive poses. I loved my fans, but they could be demanding. More then a few even groped me as we coupled together for "the shot of a lifetime." I smiled and laughed, and made it seem like great fun, but it took its toll on me.

Somehow I made it through the Convention, only to fall into bed back in Los Angeles for a long rest. My days of getting out of bed and going to work became fewer and fewer. I began having hemorrhoid problems, which resulted in my going to the hospital for surgery. The procedure, which was simple, didn't concern me. What did was keeping my identity secret. That wasn't always easy since I was recognized almost every place I went. The confidentiality of medical records meant little. If a nurse or an orderly or someone in the hospital were to find out that John Holmes was a patient, there was a good chance that they would tell a friend, who would tell a friend, and so on, just like in the commercial.

Having everyone know that I'd had a hemorrhoid operation was no problem, only we decided instead to tell everyone that I had colon cancer, and that I had to have six feet of my intestines cut out. But we knew that if someone started digging into my recent medical history, it wouldn't be long before the real truth would be out all over "Hollyworld."

The surgery itself was successful, but by this time my immune system was so raped that I didn't know if I would ever heal. Sure, the hemorrhoids were gone but the pain was worse than before. I probably should have left the bastards alone because word did get out about me. Now the press was banging at my door, wanting to know if it was true that I had cancer - or did if I really have AIDS?

"AIDS?" I said with a tone of disbelief that they were even asking me this question. "NO WAY," was my reply. "I have cancer," I tried my best to convince them.

I probably shouldn't have admitted to anything because I soon started to feel better, well enough to even consider working again. During the fall of 1986, I was invited to Italy to star in three adult films. The deal was for three weeks at top dollar, first class all the way, all expenses paid. Ordinarily I'd have been packed within the hour, but several tempting opportunities to work at home had also come along. I had one week to make up my mind.

After more than 20 years in the business, offers were still coming my way. I considered myself lucky, and a survivor. Most of the performers in my line had disappeared after only a handful of films, burned out or washed up. The public was after new faces, new bodies, and new thrills. I had walked a few tightropes in my time, even dodged a few bullets. Despite my shaky reputation, however, my films were selling better than ever. The demand for theatrical releases may have slipped, but the hot video market had expanded the audience, and demand, for fresh product.

It didn't take more than a few days to sort out the work offers. Whichever I chose, I knew that I would be taking the chance of giving AIDS to someone, either at home or in Italy. I thought long and hard about my decision. But I realized that whichever offer I chose, I would be working mostly with my same circle of people from the San Fernando Valley. Maybe I wasn't thinking clearly, but I figured if they didn't get AIDS from me it was likely they would get AIDS from someone else in the business. At that time, I had believed it was a local actress who had infected me. I wasn't out for revenge or to hurt anyone, I wanted only to work. Desperately.

The trip to Italy won out. Money certainly was a factor, but there was also the opportunity to see the hillsides of Italy one more time, a place I had always thought was so beautiful, had great food, and wonderful people. The clincher, however, was the opportunity of working with someone new. Her name was Ilona Staller, but she was better known as "La Ciccolina." An Italian film star, she was also a member of the Italian Parliament. The movie was to be called The Rise and Fall of the Roman Empress.

Filming in Europe can have its drawbacks. Some years earlier, while working in France, we had to shoot the entire production twice, once in English and again in French. As soon as a scene was finished in one language, we went back and did it again in another, line by line until we got it perfect. Then we went on to the next line. It was a bore, and I hadn't the foggiest idea what I was saying in French.

The Italians were 50 times more professional. They had us work straight through, in English only, then dubbed the finished product. They also stayed sober on the set. The French crew was drunk by mid-morning, and literally dropped the cameras while film was rolling.

Working with an Italian crew meant having a translator on the set. The studio furnished us with a little redhead, the cutest thing since Oreo cookies. I wanted her in the worst way, but I knew I would be putting her at risk too, so I didn't press it. Had I made a move I might have left Italy without my most strategic part. We later discovered she was a Mafia princess.

One of the benefits of filming overseas is the side trips. This time, because of the long schedule, I was able to sneak off between pictures to as many places as possible during the time available. I visited old friends in Germany, wandered Romania, Czechoslovakia and Spain.

Between work and running from place to place I had little time to relax. The pace seemed to agree with me and, for the first time in months, I felt terrific. Not even the constant changes in food, water and climate affected me. I had only one "off" day, which I blamed on a night without sleep. I knew better, but I wasn't complaining. For me to feel as good as I did was kind of a miracle. Nevertheless, I laid low for awhile. The production company simply cancelled me out that day and worked around me.

It wasn't until the shoot was about over and I was about to leave Italy that I began to really fall apart. I knew something was wrong almost immediately, but the signals kept growing stronger. It was then I decided to stop in Ohio on the way back to California to see my mother, perhaps for the last time. It had been years since we had seen each other. We hadn't even talked since she had called while I was locked up during the murder trial.

My mother is such a special lady. Through the years she even earned the name "Mother Moses" because she knew things and felt things before they happened. I had hoped to surprise her by showing up as I did. I hadn't called, written or anything to let her know I was coming. So when I rang the doorbell and she asked, "Who is it?" I replied, "Jessie James." The joke was on me when she opened the door, held out her arms, and said, "I knew you were coming, Johnny Buck."

We had a wonderful visit but a lot of things went purposely unsaid. Before leaving for Italy I needed to get a new passport. I had lost all of my personal papers during those hiding out days following the Laurel Canyon Murders, so it was necessary for me to get a copy of my birth certificate. When it arrived I was shocked to find a "Carl Estes" named as my real father, not Edward Holmes. Who was Carl Estes? I wondered. But I couldn't bring myself to question mother about him. If she had wanted me to know she would have told me long ago. The last thing I wanted to do was embarrass her, or make her feel ashamed or uncomfortable about any mistakes she may have once made. That was Ed's and Harold's little game, not mine.

The stop over in Ohio to see Mom was like an injection of miracle medicine for me. But the high of being in her company, amid familiar old surroundings, faded as the miles stretched between us on the return flight to L.A. It was difficult for me to get back into the routine of office work and my time there became very limited. Gone were the 10-12 hour days, the old dawn to dark work schedule. At first, I would cut out just after lunch and make for home. Within about three months I wasn't showing up for work at all. Screw it, I told myself. Why bother going in? I certainly wasn't accomplishing anything.

Now I feel my life is all but over. I lie in bed. I watch television. I wait for Misty to come home from work. I am in and out of sleep. I am getting more confused with each passing day.

CHAPTER 10

The days go by, and yet, time has no meaning for me. Lying in bed, I worry about money and mounting doctor bills, about the very real possibility of having to find a less expensive place to live. I worry about Misty. She comes home every night with a migraine headache. She tries to tell me the scoop for the day, but there are times when I can't keep up with her in my mind. I feel I am losing it.

My business partner continues to play games with her head. He is trying to get her in bed, she tells me. Hearing that upsets me, but I want her to be open with me, painful or not. He has been talking to the cops, she says, and she is frightened of what he might be revealing to them. Misty has been questioned by our employees who wonder why the Feds are in Bill's office. I wonder myself whom they could be asking him about! Several porn companies around the San Fernando Valley have been raided in recent weeks, yet we have had no problems. That fact alone puts terrifying thoughts in my mind. Bill has even hired his own daughter who happens to be only sixteen years old as our front secretary. If we were to get raided and she was to be found, we would all be in some serious trouble. But not as much trouble as Bill would be in if he were to implicate certain influential people. If that is the case, Misty is really in harms way.

Am I being paranoid? Worry seems to occupy most of my time these days. Worry, television and sleep. But even as I stare at the television screen in a half-stupor, my mind turns to dark thoughts. Misty tells me a "John Holmes Relief Fund" has been started to help with the medical bills, and some money has come in from longtime friends and business associates. If my story ever gets published I want these people to know how truly grateful I am to them. You know who you are. The funds have helped a great deal; my medication runs over eighty dollars a week. That amount sounds rather piddly now compared to what I used to spend on illegal drugs, but with me not working it's a real concern.

Misty and I have had to move again. Without any notice, the rent on our apartment was raised to nearly one thousand dollars a month. Impossible. Now the landlord in our new place is giving us hell about our animals. To make matters worse, my salary has been cut off at the company. My partner has told Misty that I am out; the company is his alone. What is he doing with all the incoming revenue? He is not paying me, and people are calling me at home because he has not been paying our account payables, some of whom had earlier given us credit based only on my word.

Bill won't talk to me, but I have heard from people close to me that he has told them I really don't need the money. The cash from the "Relief Fund," he is saying, is going to support my drug habit. He's right in a way. The money is buying drugs, but not the drugs of old. To take those would only intensify my pain. The drugs I take now are received legally from my doctor.

One drug, halcyon, keeps me out of it most of the time. When it doesn't seem to be taking effect, or working quickly enough, I increase the dosage without the doctor's knowledge or approval. My temper flares too much at times so I tend to take an extra dose before Misty comes home. I want to be asleep when she arrives. That way I don't have to hear about Bill and his backstabbing. That way I won't lose my temper.

I keep telling Misty to find someone else so that it will be easier for her when I'm gone, but the girl sticks by me no matter how much I take my pain and anger out on her. Living with me right now has to be the most difficult thing, and I really wouldn't blame her if she did hook up with another man, a guy who would not only care for her but also treat her as she deserves to be treated. I assure her that I will still love her no matter what she decides to do because I want her to be happy, and she can't be happy with me, not the way I am right now.

I look at her and see so much confusion in her eyes. It was easier for her when I guided her through everything that went on at work. Now everything has changed. She comes home so stressed with questions that I can't or don't know how to answer. I can only offer guidance for her to seek peace. But my mind is such these days that I have a difficult time doing even that for her. I am at my "best," for want of a better word, while she is at work believing I am asleep. It is then I call on every bit of energy I can muster to put these final thoughts on tape. I guess you might say that this is my last "shot." I wonder if Misty will ever find these truths that for some reason I am compelled to put into words.

Another day, another crisis. The time has come for Misty to sever all ties with my partner, Bill. At this point I don't know which has been more stressful for her, the company or me. I do know she has quit, and papers will be served this week. I told her to make copies of everything in her office before she left. I might not be around when the lawsuit goes to trial, so it is important for her to have all records available to her, especially since she was the company bookkeeper. No telling what Bill might pull when it comes to the unpaid accounts and his own creative bookkeeping. Whatever money we may win, whether I'm still here or not, will go to Misty. She deserves all she can get for working so hard and putting up with all the shit.

It pains me to think of what Misty is about to face. I will be of no help to her, but she says she will hang in there as long as she can. One thing is certain. The minute Bill finds out about the lawsuit, everything will come to an end, including my insurance coverage. How will we pay for the doctors, hospital visits, lab tests, and medications? I can't imagine not having medical insurance right now. How will we pay for anything with Misty no longer working?

The thought of suicide has crossed my faltering mind more than once. Suicide is tempting, not to be free of agony but for money. I've done just about everything else for pay, why not suicide? If I decide to end it all, my life insurance policy will still be honored, and Misty will collect one hundred thousand dollars, enough to set her up for a few years at least. How I would love to make her life easier, and how easy it would be for me to do just that. Only one thing stops me: my mother. I know it would kill her for me to take the cowardly way out, despite the absence of all hope. She wouldn't see it that way, but that is how I look at it.

Strange that Misty should be thinking of mother, too. She wants me to get in touch with mother and the rest of my family, even my little brother, David. Since my time is near I want to give a lot of my belongings to them, a piece of me so they won't forget. Actually, Misty has already started the giveaway. Before she quit the company she took some of my belongings to work and shipped them from the warehouse, following instructions to black out the names and addresses in the UPS book. That is a lesson I had learned when Nash got a hold of my address book. With everything coming to a head there, I didn't want to take any chances. That was okay with Misty even though letting go was - and is - hard on her. Many of the things I have been giving away hold special meaning for her too, but she is being a good sport about it. I just hope she understands why I must do this for my family.

Mother arrived yesterday. She is with me now and it is wonderful to have her here. I checked myself into the Veterans Hospital a couple of days ago. At least now, my pain is lessened from the morphine shots. The Veterans Administration has offered to pay for AZT medication, but I have declined. Why delay the inevitable? Mother and Misty are getting along great together. There was a time when I wondered if Mother would like Misty. Not any more. How could she not like her?

I hear them talking. Misty has been asking mother about my childhood and mother is full of stories, some I've never heard before. Maybe I have, but very little makes sense now. Everything seems so long ago and so far away, almost as if she is speaking about someone else. I was a special child, Mother says. I had a gift of making everyone laugh, even in the worst of times. Her voice is soft, warm and loving.

"I have never regretted bringing John into this world," Mother confesses, "even though the circumstances in which John was born were difficult. That's why I could never blame him for the way he lived his life. I could never do that."

Hearing Mother say those words has brought me a calmness I haven't felt for many years. It's wonderful to know that she has come to accept things that before she couldn't even understand. She may have never approved, and that's fine. Her acceptance is all I need.

How lucky I am. I am suddenly at peace with myself, in the company of the two people I love more than anything in the world. They are such an important part of my life, and so very special to me.

Lady Blue

Tho it seems ten lifetimes, it has only been
ten months.

And each day J spend less hours thinking
of the things we've lost.

Jt is only in the night when my thoughts are
not my own.

When J can t control my feelings - when my
heart begins to roam.

Jt's these hours that J am sleeping that my
love returns to you.

Can't J let go these feelings --
Oh, how J love thee, Lady Blue.

The Charm of Youth

When one grows old, his channels of interest are few:
money, sex, security. But to be young and curious
about everything is the energy and charm of youth
whose searchings for knowledge sate the thirsts of
those who have found out such is the social
structure of a race of beings still as surely locked
into it's primal past as those poor creatures whose
own carrion fuel those who would devour it's flesh, is
it wrong that like the mole who digs or bird that
flys, we develope our particular talent for survival,
but unlike the mole who learns to dig, then learns no
more or bird that is what is our gift leads us to
learn. To learn, to seek and find is to fail – is to seek
no more – is to teach those who seek – to fail there
is no absolutes to seek to find to seek to improve.
Forever is never to lose the charm of youth.

EPILOGUE

By Laurie Holmes (*Misty Dawn*)

J ohn was right. The worst was yet to come for both of us. With AIDS came encephalitis, swelling of the brain. With encephalitis came periodic seizures. Between the halcyon and the encephalitis, John would often black out; other times he would become enraged and out of control. The man I once knew was already dead. I couldn't bear to see him in such agony and pain. It was during those darkest of times I knew I had to take complete charge, not just of John but of everything. My "Daddy" was gone. He was still with me physically but no longer could I turn to him for help or advice. From here on, I told myself, I could only hope for the best.

Something inside told me it would be best to drop the lawsuit against Bill. The loss of the company meant little when I was facing the loss of the man I loved so much. And with John fading so quickly, I knew that if the lawsuit got nasty, I would be the one to have to face the attacks from everyone who had a problem with it, meaning that if the lawsuit were to occur and the companies assets were frozen, then the company would not be able to pay its debts. This could have put me in a dangerous situation.

There were times when I wanted John to die as much as he wanted to die. Actually, I felt pretty dead myself most of the time. Nearing the end of the summer of 1987, when John began failing so quickly and was urging me to leave the company, I had known it was time for me to get out. Finding a new job wasn't so hard, but having Bill cancel John's medical insurance certainly was. I had been through hard times before and I would do anything necessary to survive, but watching John have to give up his animals was unbearable. They were such an important part of his life; in many ways, one of the few remaining ties to the "country boy" days of his life. If only I could have spared him that anguish. But we were forced to move into another apartment that didn't allow animals. We thought we could get away with sneaking in our cat, T.C. - short for Titty Kitty - but we were caught.

The last time I saw any real excitement on John's face was October 1, 1987. It had been unusually hot the past couple of weeks, but it was early morning and John had just awakened, raging with fever when the earthquake hit. Leave it to an earthquake to make John laugh at the fear of danger, and to make him come alive one last time. Maybe it was because he wasn't the least bit frightened of death at that point. What was the worst that could happen to him? It wasn't many days later that John realized the time had finally come for him to check into the Veteran's Administration Hospital in Sepulveda, California. I visited him nearly everyday at first, but between working and going to the hospital at night, I was near collapse. John told me not to come see him at all, but to go out and have fun and live it up for him. "You'll meet someone," he said, "someone who will make it easier for you when that 'glorious day' comes and I'm gone."

I really didn't understand why he kept pushing me to meet someone, not at first anyway, but after a time I knew. He was watching me die just as I was watching him die. The only difference was, I was still alive and healthy. Even so, I never could tell when he was serious or delirious. There were times when he made absolutely no sense at all. He once insisted that President Reagen was outside his window. "Run for cover," he warned. "The government is trying to bomb me."

I calmed him down, then all but forgot about the episode until recently. Thinking back, John might not have been so far from the truth. Perhaps the bomb he was hallucinating about had already hit him. Why? Because nobody who had been with John, including myself, had come down with AIDS.

What makes me wonder is the fact that John and Bill went

to Washington D.C. right around the time John would have contracted AIDS. It was also during the time that Edward Meese and his "Meese Commission" were on a crusade to shut down the porn industry. I remember hearing that Meese showed President Reagan some porn movies at the White House, one of which I was in. Then along came John and Bill and a few others to fight City Hall, so to speak. John even met one of Reagan's Secret Service men. Could it be that John Holmes was injected or somehow given a strain of the AIDS virus? Maybe it was the United States Government, not God, making an example of John to underscore the "horror" of pornography. Who better to use as an example than "The King of Porn" himself?

John was in the V.A. Hospital for the last five months of his life. His basement room had only one window, up toward the ceiling, so it provided no view and little outside light. It was a large room, painted a dull powder blue, almost a wedgewood color. Nice for dishes but not a hospital room. His bed was pushed against the far wall, giving the room a stark, empty feeling. I never knew what state of mind John would be in when I visited. Just being in the "Blue Room" was enough to depress anyone.

The V.A. tried several times to give John AZT, but he had told me earlier he didn't want to prolong his death so I made them stop giving it to him. John simply wanted to die, and I wanted to make sure he died as comfortably as possible. He didn't eat much of anything except Super Sugar Crisp cereal, which I brought from home. As long as he had his cereal, cigarettes and morphine shot, he was comfortable. With assistance, he could get out of bed and walk slowly to the bathroom, which was across that long room and down the hall. Then, after a few weeks, that became impossible for him and he needed a wheelchair. The doctors had told me several times that he wouldn't last much longer, maybe only days, but John kept going. He should have died several times, and he didn't. I think he wanted to make sure I would be okay.

I had tried to keep John's whereabouts secret. That was possible for awhile, but once word got out the phone began ringing. John wasn't up to talking with anyone about anything. And I really didn't want people to see him in such poor condition. There were a few exceptions, of course, his family and a few close friends, but I had to refuse anyone else and instructed the hospital to admit no one without my approval. One day, however, I got a call from a nurse at the V.A., to tip me off that the cops were on their way. The nurse didn't say but it was obvious what they wanted: a death bed confession from John regarding the Laurel Canyon Murders. I raced to the car and headed for the freeway, breaking every traffic law possible to make it to the hospital before Detective Tom Lang and his team got there. Even if John had wanted to say what he thought might have happened on Wonderland Drive, I knew his mind was such that he could very well say what never happened. And for John to say something stupid might put me in danger or even sign my own death warrant.

Thank God I reached John's bedside before the police did. "The cops are on the way," I told him hurriedly. "When they arrive pretend to be 'out of it.' SAY NOTHING." At that moment I could hear footsteps coming down the long corridor. "This is it, John," I said. "It's showtime."

Just like a scene in an old-time movie, John reached over, put out his cigarette and probably gave the most convincing performance of his life.

When Detective Lang couldn't get anything but moaning out of John, he turned to me. John was looking at me out of the corner of his eyes. I knew that look. He was telling me to be careful. Anything I said might be twisted or taken out of context.

I told Detective Lang the truth. John had never said much to me about what had happened in Laurel Canyon. Even if John had wanted to go into it with me, I probably would have told him that I didn't want to know. I still don't want to know who killed those people, but knowing a part of

John that most people didn't, I can honestly say that the few things he did mention made sense. His compassion for people would have compelled him to go through the house on Wonderland to make sure there wasn't anyone who needed help. There was also a very good possibility that John would be the next victim, or so he believed, and a survivor could give him a clue as to who might be after him.

John was already more involved in what had taken place than he had ever wanted to be. If someone had been out to get him, or set him up for the murders, he knew he had better gather as many facts as possible. Besides, John was still under the impression that Eddie Nash's men were waiting for him outside, and that Nash wanted John to bring back what had been stolen from him. What John saw as he wandered from room to room in that slaughterhouse, and described to the Grand Jury, is undoubtedly what got him cleared.

From the few things that John had told me about Nash, I'm glad I never met the man. I'd had several opportunities, even before I knew John. A friend of mine, a photographer, rented space for a studio above one of Nash's nightclubs on Hollywood Boulevard, across from the Chinese Theatre. The chance of running into Nash was pretty good, yet it never happened. On one occasion, during the time that John was still in jail, again before I knew John, an associate of Nash's asked me if I wanted to meet Nash. By this time Nash's name had been all over the news, and not only known in inner circles. "Hell, no, I don't want to meet him," I answered quickly.

Years later, after Nash got out of jail, John and I had to go on 24-hour watch for several weeks. John was terrified beyond belief, so I didn't dare fall asleep on my watch. It was a frightening and seemingly endless time.

John was also afraid of someone else, one of the people associated with the Laurel Canyon "family." He was a master of disguise, John said, insisting that if anyone ever came to our door and pretended to be a cop, flashing a badge or not, that I was to grab the gun and call the L.A.P.D. "Verify the guy's name and badge number, and the reason why he was there," he told me. John was especially adamant about following these instructions, which he repeated to me often through the years.

Looking back on everything he had said, and knowing things now that I didn't know then, I would have to guess that the person John so feared was the man he called "Killer Karl." John seemed much more frightened of him than Eddie Nash, but I didn't realize that until several months after Nash was released from jail. I had received a phone call from my photographer friend wanting to know if I knew how to contact John. At that time, only a few people knew we were living together, so I told my friend that I might be able to locate him, but I had to know why. He then told me that Nash's brother needed to talk to John, and he gave me a phone number to give John should I see him. The odd thing was that John didn't hesitate to call Nash's brother. And while I didn't hear the conversation, I could sense a change in John's attitude toward Nash. John never lost his fear of "Killer Karl," however.

During the filming of one of my movies in which John had a scene, I accidentally discovered that we were going on location to Eddie Nash's building in Hollywood, where I used to visit my photographer friend. The thought of going back to that place frightened me, but I didn't want to say anything to Bill or anyone else on the set that day for the fear they might have thought I knew more than I really did about Nash. But I couldn't hide my fear. For John's safety, I had to tell them, not only about Nash's nightclub but his thugs who were always hanging around and packing heavily. Long before I met John, I was in the club when a big black man grabbed me from behind and started to fondle me. I broke away, called him a dirty name, and disappeared. But I never forgot his face. A couple of years ago, I was looking at a newspaper article in the Los Angeles

<u>Times</u> that a friend had sent to me. There, in a photo, was that face again. It belonged to Gregory Diles, Nash's right hand man and bodyguard.

Looking back, I believe what shocked me most about that film location was that Bill and the people connected with this movie hadn't known about Nash's building, but I did. And while the site for that day's location was changed to another location, I had to wonder who had recommended Nash's spot to them in the first place, especially since John was involved in all their projects at that time. John had told me that he and Nash had come to an understanding after he had talked with Nash's brother. I've never known what that conversation was about, but "Killer Karl" never showed his face in town again.

The mention of "Killer Karl's" name not only petrified John; it brought a silent look of terror to other faces as well, including Bill. How strange then that the police never suspected "Killer Karl" in the murders. This man must have had strong connections somewhere. He certainly had access to every type of uniform imaginable. And he was known as a person that enjoyed torturing people to death, according to John.

I guess the "Laurel Canyon Murders" is one case that will be left to a court much higher than any in California. I truly believe that the guilty, whoever he or they are, will have to answer to God himself. Even if the killer or killers believed the Wonderland people were scum, they themselves had to be truly evil to do such a job in that manner.

The only thing I really know for sure about the murders is that if John had really participated in killing those people, he could have never died with such a peaceful look in his eyes. I saw that look because I am the one who tried to shut his eyes when he died, but they wouldn't stay shut. I sat for hours in the "blue room" staring into them before the coroner came.

After John died, Nash and Diles were charged with the gruesome murders, thanks in part to the testimony given to the police by Liberace's ex-lover who claimed to have been at Nash's house the night the murders took place. John had often spoken of the existence of the "Lavender Hill Mob," supposedly a group of gay mobsters in Los Angeles. John knew about this "family" because he admitted to have run drugs for them. God only knows why Liberace's lover was hanging out with Nash, who, along with Diles, was subsequently involved in two trials. The first ended in a mistrial and the second in acquittal for both men. Liberace died of AIDS in 1987. According to a recent newspaper article I saw, the police apparently still harass Nash. It said they seized a mothball thinking it was an eight ball of meth.

John thought that he had said good-bye to his Mother for the very last time on his way back from Italy, but she had sensed something was wrong during his visit and for the last few months of his life, she was with him every step of the way. I was very grateful, not just to have her there for John, but for the time she and I got to spend together. What I learned from her about John's early years was that, while no family is perfect, John had a very loving family whose love endured despite any embarrassment or ill feelings from days gone by. These people were not the "white trash" that Hustler Magazine implied they were in a tasteless article about John following his death. Then again, Hustler was wrong about a lot of things in that article.

I don't know what I would have done without John's Mom. To see her at his bedside seemed to give me strength. But by then I was so emotionally and physically drained that all I wanted to do was have fun again. Everything John had told me about going on with my life was beginning to have real meaning. Although I loved him, and I still do, he needed his Mother more at that point than he needed me. It was like when I get sick, even today, I want my Mommy!

Those last weeks were so difficult for John. He was really frustrated because he could not complete a sentence without forgetting what he was trying to say. His legs ached constantly, especially lying motionless in bed. Often I would find him slumped in his wheelchair out in the courtyard, soaking up the sun, seeking the light as if the sun were God Himself. One thing I could always say about John, even during his darkest moments, was that he had class and charisma. As poorly as he felt and looked, he treated the nurses like ladies, even the ones who were not always on time with his painkilling morphine. Despite his dreadful condition, he had those women wrapped around his fingers. It appeared that they liked John a lot. He might have been half-dead, but he never lacked charm, right up to his dying day. Maybe that is why one of the nurses had tipped me off when Detective Lang was out for a deathbed confession. Looking back on the O.J. Simpson trial, I wonder if that same nurse remembered Detective Lang's visit to John's bedside. I certainly do, and I wasn't at all shocked the way the L.A.P.D. mishandled those proceedings. John had always insisted that the L.A.P.D. was as crooked as they came. Of course, that was John's opinion.

It was a Friday evening, and it had been a long, tiring week. Maybe it was bad timing, but for once in a very long time I actually had plans to go out with some friends I had met at work. I was very much looking forward to the evening, but when I arrived home from the office there was a message from John's Mom saying that he had lapsed into a coma. The worried sound of her voice troubled me even more than hearing that John was comatose. This wasn't the first time he had slipped into a coma, and I was certain he would pull out of it just as he had in the past. Ironically, I had just bought a brand new black dress for the evening, so I wore it to the hospital. I figured I would see John before going out with my friends.

When I entered John's room, his Mom and his half-brother, David were at his bedside. I walked over to them and looked down at John. At that moment his eyes slowly opened, almost as if he was waiting for me to say good-bye.

He looked at me and said in a faint voice, "You look very nice in that dress." Somehow he knew that the dress was new and that I had bought it for a special time, even though I had not really bought it with him in mind.

I stayed with John for some time, and all the while he remained awake and alert. Finally, I felt it was safe to leave for the evening. Maybe I should have stayed, but somehow I felt he wanted me to go. Then, too, maybe he didn't want to see the look on my face as he left this world.

Although John had shown surprising resilience throughout my visit, he certainly wasn't strong enough to sit up in his hospital bed, even slightly. But as I left his room and stood in the doorway, he suddenly raised himself up. Where he found the strength, I don't know, but there he was, propped up without any support.

"I love you, Daddy," I said, choking back the words.

And then he spoke. I remember his words and the way he said them just like it was yesterday. "I know," he replied softly, "and I love you, baby."

I turned quickly and the door shut behind me. Then I began the walk down that long, desolate corridor. I wanted to cry; I wanted to run. All I could do was wonder how I could face what was surely about to happen. I knew it wouldn't be long before I would have more to deal with than I could ever possibly handle.

I went out that night and tried to act as if I hadn't a care in the world. I was determined to have fun, possibly for the last time. And that is just what I did. Maybe the evening was so enjoyable because I felt John still with me, the two us having a great time the way we once did. I know that's the way he would have wanted it to be. Fun without worry, fun without guilt. He had been so proud of the way I grown up and taken charge of everything when he couldn't. I certainly didn't want to let him down or have him think I couldn't handle my emotions once he was gone.

Sometime during that evening John fell into another

coma. This time he didn't open his eyes when I stood beside him early the next morning. The slight rise and fall of his chest was the only indication that he was still with us.

On the way to see John, I had stopped at a music store to buy a cassette to play for him. I had heard the song on the radio several times the week before, and everything that this song was saying was truly how I felt. I thought it was only right that I should play it for him. The song was called "Everything I Own" by a group named Bread. That evening, his Mother and I went back to my apartment so exhausted that we both fell immediately to sleep. It wasn't much later that the phone rang. We both knew who was calling, and why. Neither of us rushed to the phone. We simply stood looking at one another for a moment.

When we got to the hospital and entered John's room, I sensed an overwhelming presence. John's body was dead, but his spirit was waiting for me. I looked at him, then up toward the ceiling, and said, "Go now, John, go to the light. Don't worry, I'll be okay. I'll take care of everything." With that his presence was gone.

John had died with his eyes open. I tried to shut them, but they wouldn't stay shut. Still, there was a peace about him, and the look in his eyes seemed to say he had looked right at death and said, "Take me, I'm yours." It was that look in his eyes that told me once and for all that he had not killed those people in Laurel Canyon. Anyone that could have committed such a horrifying act of multiple murders and mayhem could never have a look like that when facing death.

John's Mom and I waited at least five hours for the men from the mortuary to arrive at the hospital. Meanwhile, we had our own little ceremony. John had always made it very clear he didn't want a funeral or anything even close to one. I'm sure he didn't mind just the two of us doing what we did. It was very private, and it helped to make the long wait a peaceful one, and surprisingly bearable. Then the people from the mortuary finally showed up. Seeing those men wheel John's body down the corridor was unnerving, mainly because the body bag appeared to have no body in it. That's how much - or how little - of John was left. Then it was just John's Mother and myself. We quickly left the V.A. Hospital and drove back to my apartment. When morning finally came I took her to David's house. Suddenly I realized I was truly alone. My "Daddy" was gone forever.

I never thought I could feel so alone, but I did. The "glorious day" had finally come for John, and although I knew I had to go on, my future felt so empty. I cried my heart out into my pillow that whole day until, finally, late in the afternoon, my doorbell rang. It startled me. I couldn't imagine who could be at my door since so few people knew where I lived. Cautiously, I looked thought the peephole and saw a man with flowers. Never having seen this person before, I grabbed my gun and slowly opened the door. I hid the gun behind my back as I reached for the flowers, but I was so distraught I never realized that the delivery man could see it in the mirror directly behind me.

The flowers set me off again. At this point, I knew I couldn't be alone for one more minute, so I called David and told him I was on my way over. We were watching the news when a reporter started talking about John's death. I knew John would make the news that night, but what I heard the reporter saying about my beloved husband was more then I could possibly handle. According to "an unnamed source," John had died of AIDS, which he had contracted from using needles. When I heard that, I hit the roof with rage. I was on the phone to the network immediately to correct the story. But I think the truth was less surprising to the people there than to hear that John had a "secret wife." In gathering the information for their report they had not found a clue that John was married.

What I told the network reporter, and the others that followed in numerous interviews, was the absolute truth. I went into even more detail during an appearance on the

Larry King Show. "John did not get AIDS from dirty needles," I told King and his television audience. "John was first tested for AIDS in 1985 and was HIV negative. He was tested again in 1986 and was HIV positive. In between, John had starred in six or seven films, all heterosexual. He did not go to parties; he was basically a homebody. What I did not tell the world, was that John had gone to the White House during the time that he would have contracted AIDS, to defend his industry.

"Some people in the industry have said that it is safer to have sex in the business than in the 'real world' because porn actors and actresses practice 'safe sex.' I could never say 'safe sex' was being practiced in pornography. In fact, anything but! Most actors and actresses are very transient, traveling back and forth between Los Angeles, San Francisco and New York. Even if they have been tested a day or a week before shooting a film, who knows where they have been between the test and the start of a film. A lot of them have sex for money on the side, using their fame to make even more money. Most of them are on drugs. So there's a lot of action going on, both in front of and behind the camera.

"Remember, it takes four to sixteen weeks for the HIV antibodies to show up in a person's blood. It's simply not realistic to believe that testing gives an accurate account of anyone's current HIV status."

I 'm sure that what I had to say before Larry King and the others pissed a few people off, but I was telling it like it really was at the time. Besides, I didn't care what anyone thought. I was angry, and I had been angry ever since a story had appeared in the paper prior to John's death that he had AIDS because of a drug habit. I know who leaked that garbage to the press and why. I also know who had contacted the network news right after John's death. I simply couldn't let it go down that way. It wasn't right.

It was John's wish to be cremated, and he was adamant that I view his body just before it went into the furnace. He wanted me to make sure that a part of him - his most famous part - was still intact; he didn't want it to end up on a shelf in a jar as a "conversation piece" or collectible. My legs were like lead as I walked into the crematorium. I didn't want to see John again, not that way, but I had to make good my promise to him.

John was lying on a table, naked. I walked over to him and, thank God, his body was still intact. I don't know what I would have done if it hadn't been. Then I placed a picture of Jesus that he had once given to me on his chest and watched as his body went into the fire. I stayed for a little while, gasping my every breath, wanting to be anywhere except where I was, knowing what was happening to his body inside the furnace.

Later that night I picked up John's ashes and took them to David's house. Another of John's wishes was to have David drill holes in the urn. Once that was done he placed tape over the openings. That evening I slept with the urn containing John's ashes in the bunk of a well-known fishing barge, a boat that John and I had often fished from around the Channel Islands.

We left Oxnard, California that evening around eleven o'clock. I slept with John's Mother, his brother and God knows how many fishermen were in the bunks at the bottom of the boat. I clung to John's ashes as if they were truly sacred. Then around four-thirty that morning, we awoke to do our deed. I had a cup of coffee and by five o'clock we walked toward the back of the boat, peeled the tape off the urn and without a spoken word I threw the urn into the water on the other side of San Clemente Island. The water was so deep, blue and unpolluted, just as John wanted it to be. We fished those waters the rest of the day. I think John would have wanted that, too.

Before we returned to shore that evening, a young girl came up to me. She was part of the crew that helped in the galley. She had recognized me from the news, and told me that she was sorry for my loss. While handing me a single red rose, she said, "This is for John." I starred out into the ocean and then tossed it into John's watery grave.

Several hours later, as our boat pulled up to dock, I noticed two men watching us. They weren't doing anything, just standing and staring, but they frightened me. For some reason they seemed out of place. We hurried to the car, acting as if we hadn't noticed them. It was a relief to leave them behind.

I was on the road again two weeks later, this time by myself. I drove out of town in the car that John had bought me for my 24th birthday with a U-haul trailer attached, "flipping off" Los Angeles as I headed over the hills and away from the San Fernando Valley. I had to get away. Like John, I was beginning to feel people were after me. I was in such a state the night before, in fact, that I had slept in my car with John's gun, fearing that all of my worldly goods, such as they were, might be stolen.

Once back in my hometown, I felt great. With the insurance money from John's policy, I bought a house in a small suburb, thinking that I would spend the rest of my life there. I honestly believed that once I left Los Angeles everything would turn around for me. It did for awhile. A new man came into my life and we had a pretty good relationship. Then things began to sour. The guy stalked me for two years, after telling the whole town where I had come from and to whom I was related. It began with phone calls; over thirty life-threatening messages were left on my message machine. When he showed up at my door, tried to break in, I confronted him with the gun John had left me. He ran down the street, and I called the police. When the police arrived at my house, I played the taped messages for them. One of the officers demanded that I hand the tape over to him; if I refused, he said, the police would never again respond to a call from me. I did, and the tape strangely disappeared.

It wasn't until after my arm was broken during another incident that the police really did anything to help me, and that was only because there were witnesses and they had no choice. By then it had become real obvious that they didn't want the widow of John Holmes, "The Porn King," living in their town. If the police were not harassing me, the people of the town were. People who had once been my friends, turned their backs on me, even some of my neighbors who had once been warm and kind. At times I felt as if I were living in a Gothic novel, or, at the very least, a Communist-run community. It became very obvious that I had to sell my house if I were ever to have any peace. What bothered me most was that these people were so small-minded. They hated me because they thought I would bring pornography into their little town, raping and murdering their children along the way. Wives feared that their husbands were looking at my legs on a hot day because I wore shorts and, oh God, if they were looking at my legs, what next? Their totally messed up attitude was based not on what they knew about John or me, but what they <u>didn't</u> know. They were judging John and me because we had been involved in the Adult Entertainment Industry. Yet, a few years earlier, they had busted a mortuary in this very same town for filming teenagers having sex with corpses. As it turned out, this particular town had been chosen for the Witness Protection Program some years earlier, which would explain the attitude I received from the police and other city officials.

It has taken many years for me to get over everything, to be able to face the facts as they really are instead of how I had once perceived them to be at the time. John wasn't the God I thought he was, but then, he wasn't the demon others tried to make him out to be either.

Most people who really knew John will always love and miss him. I know I will. And I will always be grateful to the people who sent money to the John Holmes Relief Fund, such as Gloria Leonard, Annie Sprinkle, Suze Randall, Ron

Vogul and Caballero Productions. It made John feel really good that they and others cared. I still have the notes and letters that accompanied their donations. Of course, Hustler Magazine claimed that no one ever sent any money. Hustler should have checked the facts more closely before printing such garbage. Some things will never change, I guess.

Few people really understood John. In many ways he was complex, deeper than most everyone realized. When he first began working on this book, he had an idea for the title, which was **The Monkey Tree.** He told his idea to several friends and they didn't get it. They had no idea what he was talking about. So he put his explanation on paper. This is what he wrote:

In the Garden of Eden, the Bible tells us, there grew a tree with magical powers. Anyone who tasted its fruit was said to receive everlasting life.

In time the tree became a symbol of life itself; its roots representing the roots of mankind, its branches the many different directions that life can take. A tree can be shaken or struck by lightening. A limb can rot. Still, it stands strong.

Life abounds within the tree. Monkeys scamper about. Monkeys and man. We live on the lower limbs and outer reaches and soaring heights. No matter how sophisticated and intellectual we become, no matter what goals we achieve, we're all monkeys in the same tree. Reaching, falling, climbing, searching, hiding.

There's no escape from the monkey tree. We're there always, placed somewhere by our own deeds and the opinions of others.

John F. Kennedy...Hypocrites...Charles Manson...John Wayne...Jerry Falwell. Where do they live in the monkey tree?

And John C. Holmes?

I'll let you be the judge of that.

In John's own way, he was really a fascinating man. He had a good heart, but there were too many times when he was simply lost somewhere between his own reality and fantasy. No matter what anyone says about him, I will always remember the John who, despite his own pain, went out of his way to help a little old lady who was lost. The John who gave twenty dollars to a homeless person and told him to go eat a good Thanksgiving Dinner. The John who comforted a little girl after her brother had been badly hurt in a car accident. The John who went to the pound to get a dog, picked one out with every disease imaginable, bailed her out, along with her six puppies, found homes for all the pups, and spent a small fortune nursing the dog back to health. The John who was so upset because a pigeon he had tried to rescue died overnight. The John who was the first to want AIDS testing for his Industry, and was upset because his attempts at organizing such a program had failed. The John who initiated the rumor that he had intestinal cancer, not in an attempt to deny he had AIDS, but to protect the Industry. The John who put hot towels on my tummy every few minutes when I suffered from bad cramps. The John who saved me from my own self-destruction.

John may have made mistakes in his life, but as anyone who really knew him can't deny, his best asset wasn't his penis - it was his heart.

John C. Holmes
1944-1988

Laurie Holmes

(Misty Dawn)

Born in Albuquerque, New Mexico where she lived until moving to Las Vegas, Nevada at eighteen, Laurie Rose met producer Ray Steckler who cast her in her first film role *"The Best Little Cathouse in Las Vegas."* A natural born exhibitionist, Misty Dawn was a diminutive, sensual treat whose inclination for uninhibited sexing landed her roles in such classic Adult Films as *Naughty Nurses, California Valley Girls, Desire, Girls on Fire, Naughty Cheerleaders* and *Girls Together*. Misty Dawn was in over 30 feature films and a myriad of loops and still photographs. A sprightly nymph with a reputation as one of the hardest working actresses of her era, always giving 100% to her fans, Misty Dawn possessed a most delightfully appealing figure, crowned with brown, curly hair she tossed about with unassuming lustfulness.

At 20, Laurie met the legend, John C. Holmes, on a set in San Francisco and a loving relationship ensued. With John the last five years of his life, Laurie cared for him after he contracted the AIDS virus until his admittance to the Veterans Hospital five months prior to his death. During those years, Laurie worked with John on his memoirs, now his autobiography – *Porn King*. Abandoning the adult film industry at her late husband's request, Laurie shot a couple of photo layouts in Chic Magazine. As office Manager for Penquin Productions, Laurie proved to be an astute business woman becoming Bookkeeper and Vice President of the company.

After John's death, heartbroken, Laurie moved back to her beloved home state of New Mexico where she lived a quiet life before returning to the adult entertainment industry as a dancer in local clubs. Like her film career, as an erotic dancer, Laurie tantalized her fans with a natural ability as well as unabashed sensuality. Classy, with a sardonic, intelligent, uninhibited sexuality, Laurie displayed the same sweet disposition that endeared her during her earlier career. "I just figure, if I can bring people out of my closet – theirs is a piece of cake!"

President and CEO of Johnny Wadd Inc., her company dedicated to the memory of her late husband John, Laurie Holmes distributes the book Porn King, as well as many of John's most popular films, including a number of the "Johnny Wadd" series. Visit The Official John C. Holmes website at www.johnnywadd.com. Plans for the future include an on-line advice-chat column where fans can download film clips plus an on-line publication.

Whatever Laurie Holmes dares to dream, you can count on her approaching it with the same eagerness and revelry she exhibited in her films.

Partial List of the many John Holmes major films and videos.

All night long [1975]
Always ready [1981]
Angel in mr. Holmes [1988]
Aphrodesiac [1971]
Around the world with Johnny Wadd [1975]
Aunt Peg [1980]
Aunt Peg's fulfillment [1981]
Autobiography of a flea [1976]
Baby sister [1973]
Backdoor romance [1985]
Backing in [1990]
Balling for dollars [1980]
Bedtime video 1 [1984]
Bedtime video 3 [1984]
Bedtime video 4 [1984]
Best of Gail Palmer [1981]
Best of John Holmes [1984]
Beyond fulfillment [1974]
Big melons 13 [1988]
Bigger the better [1986]
Black silk stockings [1979]
Black widow's nest [1976]
Blonde Emanuelle [1978] [3D]
Blonde fire [1979] [rape]
Blonde in black lace [1973]
Blue vanities 3 [1987]
Blue vanities 4 [1987]
Blue vanities 5 [1987]
Blue vanities 10 [1992]
Blue vanities 14 [1993]
Blue vanities 15 [1993]
Blue vanities 16 [1987]
Blue vanities 17 [1992]
Blue vanities 34 [1988]
Blue vanities 39 [1988]
Blue vanities 42 [1988]
Blue vanities 43 [1992]
Blue vanities 44 [1992]
Blue vanities 45 [1988]
Blue vanities 46 [1988]
Blue vanities 48 [1988]
Blue vanities 49 [1992]
Blue vanities 52 [1993]
Blue vanities 55 [1988]

Blue vanities 57 [1988]
Blue vanities 58 [1988]
Blue vanities 62 [1988]
Blue vanities 65 [1988]
Blue vanities 68 [1988]
Blue vanities 77 [1988]
Blue vanities 117 [1994]
Blue vanities 125 [1992]
Blue vanities 243 [1995]
Blue vanities 244 [1995]
Blue vanities 276 [1997]
Body candy [1978]
Body lust [1969]
Body shop [1984]
Bottoms up! series 2 [1978]
Bottoms up! series 4 [1978]
California gigolo [1979]
California girls [1980]
California valley girls [1983]
Candy girl [1978]
Candy Samples video review [1984]
Candy's candy [1976]
Carnal encounters of the barest kind [1978]
Casanova [1976]
Casanova 2 [1982]
Champ [1980]
Chastity and the starlets [1986]
Chastity Johnson [1986]
Cheri [1971]
China cat [1978]
Classic Swedish erotica 4 [1986]
Classic Swedish erotica 5 [1986]
Classic Swedish erotica 6 [1986]
Classic Swedish erotica 8 [1986]
Classic Swedish erotica 11 [1986]
Classic Swedish erotica 13 [1986]
Classic Swedish erotica 14 [1986]
Classic Swedish erotica 16 [1986]
Classic Swedish erotica 19 [1986]
Classic Swedish erotica 21 [1986]
Classic Swedish erotica 22 [1986]
Classic Swedish erotica 26 [1987]

Classic Swedish erotica 32 [1987]
Coming Holmes [1986]
Coming of Angie [1972]
Confessions of a teenage peanutbutter
  freak [1975]
Country girls [1975]
Cream rinse [1976]
Critic's choice [1984]
Critic's choice 2 [1984]
Cumshot revue 1 [1983]
Cumshot revue 2 [1985]
Cumshot revue 5 [1989]
Danish and blue [1970] [soft]
Danish connection [1970] [soft]
Dear Pam [1976]
Deep rub [1979]
Devil in mr. Holmes [1987]
Dickman and Throbbin [1986]
Doctor I'm coming [1969]
Door to door salesman [1970]
Double exposure [1973]
Down and dirty [0]
Ebony lust [1984]
Ecstasy [1980]
Episodes of an oriental kitten [1974]
Erotic adventures of Candy [1978]
Erotic fantasies 1 [1983]
Erotic fantasies 5 [1983]
Erotic starlets 23:
Lisa DeLeeuw [1988]
Erotica collection 7 [1982]
Eruption [1977]
Evil come evil go [1972]
Executive secretary [1974]
Exhausted [1981]
Exotic French fantasies [1973]
Extreme close up [1979]
Fantasm [1975]
Fantasm comes again [1975]
Fantastic orgy [0]
Female athletes [1978]
Fire in Francesca [1977]
First annual XRCO adult film awards
  [1985]
Flesh and laces [1983]
Flesh and laces 2 [1983]
Flesh of the lotus [1972]

Flight sensations [1983]
Four women in trouble [1972]
Frankenstein [1985]
Free and foxy [1985]
French kiss [1979]
French schoolgirl [1973]
Fulfillment [1973]
Garters and lace [1980]
Ginger Lynn meets
John Holmes [1991]
Ginger Lynn the movie [1988]
Girls in the band [1976]
Girls on fire [1984]
Good the bad and the horny [1985]
Grafenberg spot [1985]
Great sex scenes 1 [1986]
Hard candy [1976] [3D]
Hard soap hard soap [1977]
Heat of the moment [1984]
Helen Bedd [1973]
Hitchhiking harlots
Homecoming [1978]
Honey buns [1987]
Honey throat [1980]
Honeysuckle rose [1981]
Hot child in the city [1979]
Hot nurses [1977]
Hot summer night [1972]
Hunter [1971]
I am always ready [1979]
I love L.A. [1987]
I love L.A. (new) [1993]
I want you [1974]
Idol [1985]
In memory of Connie [1975]
Inches for Keisha [1988]
Incredible sex-ray machine [1975]
Insatiable [1980]
Inside Desiree
Cousteau [1979]
Jade pussycat [1977]
Jawbreakers [1985]
John C Holmes -the lost films [1988]
John C Holmes -the lost films (new)
  [1993]
John Holmes and the all-star sex
  queens [1979] [soft]

John Holmes exposed [1978]
John Holmes king of X [1988]
John Holmes superstar [1980]
John Holmes the legend continues [1997]
John Holmes' lessons in love [0]
Kama Sutra '71 [1971]
Kowloon connection [1976]
Ladies bed companion [1978]
Legends of porn [1987]
Let me count the lays [1980]
Life and times of Xaviera Hollander [1973]
Lifestyles of the blonde and dirty [1987]
Limited edition 2 [1980]
Limited edition 9 [1980]
Limited edition 10 [1980]
Limited edition 17 [1980]
Limited edition 18 [1980]
Lingerie [1983]
Liquid lips [1976]
Little French maid [1981]
Little orphan Dusty [1978]
Lollipop palace [1973]
Looking for Mr. Goodsex [1985]
Lottery lust [1986]
Lottery lust (new) [1993]
Love Boccacio style [1970] [soft]
Love explosions [1975]
Love goddesses [1981]
Love in strange places [1974]
Love notes [1987]
Love scenes for loving couples [1987]
Love with a proper stranger [1973]
Lust at first bite [1978]
Lust in America [1985]
Lusty princess [1978]
Marathon [1983]
Marilyn Chambers' private fantasies [1983]
Marina vice [1985]
Marina vice (new) [1993]
Masked ball [1975]
Moments of love [1983]
Mrs. Rodgers neighborhood [1989]
My tongue is quick [1971]
Nasty nights [1989]

Nasty nurses [1983]
Naughty girls like it big [1986]
New comers [1984]
New girl in town [1974]
New York City woman [1979]
Night on the wild side [1985]
Nudes at eleven 2 [1987]
Olé [1973]
One way at a time [1979]
Only the best [1986]
Only the best of Barbara Dare [1990]
Only the best of oral [1988]
Open for business [1984]
Oral ecstasy 3 [1988]
Orgy machine [1972]
Oriental ecstasy girls [1974]
Oriental kitten [1975]
Over easy [1980]
Over sexposure [1976]
Panorama blue [1974]
Passion for blondes [1988]
Passion pit [1985]
Passion play [1984]
Peep shows: Blonde goddesses [1982]
Peep shows: J. C. Holmes [1982]
Personal services [1975]
Pizza girls [1978]
Prisoner of paradise [1980]
Private thighs [1987]
Puss o rama [1975]
Remember Connie [1978]
Return of Johnny Wadd [1985]
Return of Johnny Wadd (new) [1993]
Ride a cocked horse [1973]
Rings of passion [1976] [bi]
Rise of the Roman empress [1987]
Rockey X [1986]
Rocking with Seka [1980]
Rub down [1985]
Saturday night beaver [1986]
Saturday night beaver (new) [1993]
Scandal in the mansion [1985]
Scriptease [1978]
Seduction of Cindy [1980]
Seka [1988]
Seka for Christmas [1979]
Senator's daughter [1978]

Sex as you like it [1972]
Sex pageant [1978]
Sex psycho [1971]
Sex station [1975]
Sexual heights [1980]
Sheer panties [1980]
Sissy's hot summer [1979]
Smash or How to get hung [1970]
Snow honeys [1983]
Spirit of seventy sex [1976]
Starlets [1976] [3D]
Stormy [1980]
Studio of lust [1984]
Suburban satanists [1974]
Summertime blue [1978]
Superstars and superstuds [1986]
Superstars of porn 2 [1985]
Swedish erotica 1 [1981]
Swedish erotica 2 [1981]
Swedish erotica 5 [1981]
Swedish erotica 6 [1981]
Swedish erotica 7 [1981]
Swedish erotica 8 [1981]
Swedish erotica 9 [1981]
Swedish erotica 10 [1981]
Swedish erotica 11 [1981]
Swedish erotica 12 [1981]
Swedish erotica 13 [1981]
Swedish erotica 15 [1981]
Swedish erotica 16 [1981]
Swedish erotica 18 [1981]
Swedish erotica 31 [1981]
Swedish erotica 44 [1982]
Swedish erotica 65 [1985]
Swedish erotica hard 15 [1993]
Swedish erotica hard 16 [1993]
Swedish erotica hard 35 [1993]
Swedish erotica superstars featuring
  Bridgette Monet [1983]
Swedish erotica superstars featuring
Seka [1983]
Sweet Alice [1983]
Sweet captive [1979]
Sweet cheeks [1980]
Sweet Julie [1973]
Sweet punkin' [1977]
Sweet sweet freedom [1976]

Swing thing [1973]
Tapestry of passion [1976]
Taxi girls [1979]
Teenage cowgirls [1973]
Teenage cruisers [1977]
Teenage fantasies 2 [1974]
Teenage lovers [1973]
Teenage madam [1977]
Tell them Johnny Wadd is here [1975]
That's erotic [1979]
That's porno [1980]
Those Lynn girls [1989]
Those young girls [1984]
Three came running [1976]
Touch [1976]
Tough cookies [1978]
Treasure box [1985]
Treasure box (new) [1993]
Tropic of passion [1979]
True legends of adult cinema: the Cult
  Supertstars [1993]
True legends of adult cinema: the
  Golden Age [1992]
True legends of adult cinema: the
  Unsung Supertstars [1993]
Ultimate pleasure [1977]
Undulations [1980]
Up 'n coming [1982]
Wet and wild [1972]
Whore of the worlds [1985]
Winning stroke [1975]
WPINK TV [1985]
Young and wet [1975]
Zolotia [1978]